Snapshots in Isolation

By

Maya Richardson, Ph.D.

Acknowledgement

To my sons, who listened

Table of Contents

The Moon and an Ab-reaction

The Moon and an Ab-re-action

The Moon, how She glowed
The Clouds, traveled as one,
As they moved all so gently
To the Darkness as One.

Initially, when I first saw the Moon, I did not sense that anything was wrong. She was the most beautiful creature I had seen that night, maybe ever. Especially the way in which, she and those two clouds moved in uniform in the northern night sky, they seemed to be inter-connected in some mysterious manner. But when they disappeared completely, all without a trace, it startled me. And in fact when they did, it jarred my senses into a conscious state of awareness. Because, before this incident, I was content to just watching it naturally disappear over the western horizon; knowing that it was doing so without any interference, except that I was watching it hoping that it would remain intact. Silly of me, I know. But that picture was quite spectacular. So when that did not occur, I thought that was okay. I will remember it in pieces. So that is where this story begins, putting together "pieces" of what I observed after that sighting disappeared.

Silence accompanied this image. And when this vibration was broken, it startled one area of the brain to listen more intently to two particular elements, the loudness factor and its depth. These two aspects of this sound signal had an association with something more than just that wind, or a shift in air temperature, they signaled danger. The sound was so intense that it struck a chord; and literally blew those silent air particles apart leaving a repercussion, a sonic boom. Which would have caught anyone's attention, even if it had not been for this after-effect, i.e., shift from silence to this noise.

These two distinctions were then compared to what were normal nocturnal sounds. For example, the chirping of crickets or the rustling of the leaves, anything that would signal that there was a range of sound that could be heard at night; which could then be compared to what had just happened . But when even these went undetected after that boom, then it seemed abnormally quiet, as though that boom and that rush of air had virtually destroyed all sound; even the silence that was there once before. But that was not possible, was it? That a sound like that could break not only what was there previously, but also slice out a chunk of air leaving it emptied and without sound. However, having heard this noise at some other time, and also in another place also informed the mind "this was not new." But it was.

This was an auditory memory which had been recognized differently than how it had been manufactured long ago, at an air show. There one expected to hear it because jets passed through airspace at astronomical speeds which broke the sound barrier, literally. Sending sound signals outward, in ripples. And when these reached us, these repercussions rattled the bones of those of us who were watching. They literally jarred our head, causing these sounds to be conducted to our inner ears where we could hear them louder. And had we not known this, then maybe the way in which that sound broke through the night air as it did, would not have startled me the way that it did. But I doubt that. And why is that? Because of the way in which that blast of air was tied into that picture of beauty. It broke the silence, but it also contributed to why it disappeared as abruptly as it did. Yet, the sound itself was also tied to a sonic blast that had been co-created by others, who wanted to destroy another's creation – the atom. So not to recognize this would be to deny it. And we all know where that leads, right? But for now, let us just stay tuned to its place in this picture, as a sound that could destroy.

When this louder emission resounded, not only did it mute the silence that was already out there, it also disrupted the hearing mechanism, the ears. They were set for silence till those soundwaves came crashing through the night, and reset them to hearing differently. That is searching for where that sound had come from, either from the north or the right, depending on one's location. And yet for the ears to remain locked into either of these positions, hearing loud sounds versus nothing at all, and only hearing them as loud or quiet, meant the ears were only honing in on what they could easily detect without discrimination. Which is all fine, well, and good; unless, one also desired to hear more than these kinds of distinctions. One desired to hear in octaves or notes. Rather than just listening for sounds or no sounds. So with that being said, it also meant the ears needed to be further attenuated.

The ears needed to recognize where they had heard that sound before, so that they could send a signal directly to the brain so it too could register it. And then respond to it. This intra-connection was not only made in a matter of a few milliseconds, but it also set the brain and the ears on fire. Attuning them both to the ramifications of having heard that sound once before; but also the image (but not this nocturnal image, a completely different one); one that should have brought forth a flood of memories with it, but it had not. And why not? If it was only a sonic blast and it just happened to have been produced out in the environment? And it seemed as innocuous as this blast of cold air that had come through this picture of beauty? Why was it not heard of in the same manner as, just smashing one atom against another inside of a vacuum?

When that soundlessness was disrupted, though, not only did it remind one of where that noise had first come from (some other side of the world), but it also set the tone, the decibel range. Not to just listen for what was no longer there (such as the silence), but to also note why that sound might have been mass produced as it was. Either this was because there was a significant amount of propulsion behind this skyward motion, and so these atoms were condensed in such a short amount of time they imploded rather than exploded; or the design of that air space contributed to the formation of these sound waves as they decombusted causing them to lengthen or shorten depending on what they happened to bump into (or not). Either way, what was heard was a drastic difference between the silence that was first occupying that air space, and what was heard afterwards, nothing; which seemed worse.

This sonic boom had cleared that space. But it also marked itself with its loudness, and its depth. Whereas being in that silent picture's motion might have carried us into sleep, this breakage reawakened us, and led us to seeing.

The eyes, however, were not convinced by this type of ear discrimination. They needed something more concrete than just listening. They wanted to see for themselves what had made that air split like it did; so to make that possible, one had to reinvent that image as it slowly moved across that open night sky. There was this very smooth lateral motion where the airspeed remained the same. Allowing for the Moon and those two clouds to be in-synch with one another as they sailed across that northern night sky all together: At ease, and seemingly at peace with one another. Then once there was this expulsion of air, and it destroyed this image, then the clouds were freed from their earlier movement; however, not without conditions. Because when they were knocked out of their earlier two positions, they were pushed in opposition to that slower moving airstream; which made the eyes suspicious.

Something was not quite right about that nocturnal vision for it to be disambulated as quickly as it was. Upon its first appearance, it looked as though it was a semi-stationary object, one which could hold one's attention to it for a very long time. And it did. However, when that vision was shifted by that nocturnal wind as it was, it was then and only then when it was recognized as a fallacy. Nothing was made permanent. And to verify this, one only had to look and confirm this. But that was just it. If the eyes had not be forewarned by the ears, i.e., by that sound, then they would have missed seeing how permanence was in question (and not just the psychological kind). This Moon and her glow, and those two clouds had gathered in that northern night sky, and were heading due west, until a part of that image was destroyed by that wind and that noise. Because before that wind came through, those two clouds were cemented to that Moon and the picture that the three of them had made. And because of this, it looked as if all of the pieces of that picture were preparing to disappear, i.e., dip down behind the western horizon together as one solid construction. But since that wind came through, and disturbed that picture of loveliness (along with that noiselessness), then no wonder when it came time for verification one needed more than just one's ear's, one needed those eyes to nab it.

Their nighttime acuity was supposed to be greater than the ears. Were they not? Because they actually caught the details quicker and were able to transmit these types of signals faster to the brain than the ears; and because they could, they also saw more than they reported. Does that make sense? It does. The ears can hear, receive all the data that they want, and even send it on to the brain because it does not disquiet the mind; but the eyes, they are restricted from this. And why is that? Because of the way they are hard-wired to the brain directly; the ears are tuned in to receive only a certain range of noises, but the eyes they see everything; but that does not translate into apprehending it all. In fact, just because they have this really unique human capability to pick-up all these light signals, and send them back to the occipital lobe, does not mean they are seeing these correctly or incorrectly. It just means they have been impinged upon. But these airwave transmissions help us to see, in the literal sense; and also "picture" what is taking place out there, i.e., comprehension. And yet, we also know that light travels faster than most sounds, right? So the eyes should have caught that wind and its commotion before the ears did; but they had not.

To the eyes all that commotion outside represented was movement. Where it looked as though there was one slow moving push toward their fait accompli, and observing it was enough, because it gave the eyes a place to rest, and to gaze upon; until there was that counter-movement. And this turned those two clouds back toward the center of that Moon, separating them forever. Because once that wind turned and moved those two clouds toward the front of that Moon, they no longer were a part of her construction; they were atmospheric accumulations. Two clouds which had been formed by Earth's day and night emissions.

No sound had accompanied them on their westward travels, and so based upon this information, when the wind shifted in the opposite direction, bringing those two clouds front and center, we should have been warned there was something amiss; but we were not. We were just curious. What happened to make that wind move in an opposing direction as quickly as it did? Especially when it looked as though that night vision was going to end on a positive note; and it did, if you happen to like barometric changes. Which happens normally at this time of night; and also in this upper atmosphere, where air currents mandate what typically happens there, and govern this area of Earth's atmosphere; not us humans. That backwards motion brought no new sound to the ear at that moment; in fact, this new motion was conducted noiselessly, only by sight. So how could that be? When just a moment ago, one was touting how sound interrupted that "noiseless nightsight," and now you are saying that was not the case at all? If the eyes were in-synch with that movement (and they were), and they also interpreted that scene as a silent motion one (and it was), then there should not have been any discrepancy between what was taking place out there through either of these two sensations, right? Wrong.

The eyes were taking in everything that was being unfolded in front of them. And this made perfect sense to them, especially since that was how they had been trained, to see the light: To pick-up everything around them that they could, and then transmit this data straight to the brain. Nothing to it right? That is what a high acuity in this visual sensory modality does; it brings in everything, light or dark. That is until something alters its visual field, then it may distort or simplify what it sees. And as I mentioned before, when that backwards motion changed that external scenery so rapidly, the eyes caught this, they shifted back to that scene as it was decomposing so that they could catch that "new" movement.

They were seeing two airwaves, one which gave them a sense of lateral knowledge, and also smoothness. This then helped the eyes to differentiate no movement, i.e., stillness, from frontwards motion which was then reversed. And then from there, know what no movement (or very little of it for the eyes to detect) meant. But here was what was so intriguing about watching from afar, one could see that airstream pick-up within a moment's notice, and literally blow those two clouds in an opposite direction. Essentially thinning it out so much that there was nothing left of it; basically, destroying it in the process. And yet, able to leave the other, bigger one intact; as though it was meant to be that way. So then, how could a wind or an airstream know not to destroy the larger one, but that it was quite all right to destroy the smaller one? And how was it that our eyes could gather that was what that wind or airstream was doing? And that we had something invested in watching that picture unfold naturally, out in space? And that we did not want it or desire it to change, before it went over the western horizon; because once it dipped below this horizon, we expected it to change. In fact, we actually counted on this. Now why is that? Because the Moon moved in her own time, separate from those two clouds, and Earth's upper atmosphere; that is why. But that did not dissuade me from watching what remained of their sight, hoping that the Moon would reappear after that, even with those two clouds still intact. Which did not make any sense whatsoever, until it was linked to a completely different scene, a blacked-out one; then, it made perfect sight sense. No vision to occupy the eyes or the mind. Nothing; which was arresting, to say the least. That is until that sonic vibration resounded once more.

Volume

In actuality this sound was a familiar one. In fact, because it was, it seemed to be more than just startling to hear that night or just a reminder of an airshow long ago. It had historical significance. And because it did, it actually reminded the ears to be on the alert. To listen more attentively than they had before; because now they remembered how that sound had been made long ago sans the entertainment piece. And how it had blasted through that clear night air, as though there was nothing to intervene or to stop it; and there was not. Once it came through, loud and clear, it continued to resonate: emitting its deep pitch in that loudness.

It was common knowledge that sound traveled to the ear, and from there it went into another sub-system where it was further differentiated into low and high decibels, tones. And also into frequencies; which could then be further distinguished by volume, from loud to nothing at all (i.e., silence). So when that sound came through (along with that wind), and that scene changed it looked as though it was doing so with sound trailing it. And on Earth that would be incorrect, because here sound travels to our ears faster than the sight. Yet, when this loud blast accompanied this change, it looked like it was in line with the producer: the east-bound wind. But it was not. The noise came from the turbulence and the decombustion of that night air. As it moved forcefully through that softer (and warmer) atmosphere. And to the eyes - when they saw what was taking place out there - they saw nothing but those two clouds, one floating along as if nothing had happened; the other, long gone.

The ears, however, knew that they were documenting this scene entirely by what they heard. And the eyes, by what they saw taking place light years away. Or at least miles from where this natural occurrence was actually taking place. But that noise? And it's rare occurrence here on Earth, and especially at that time of night, was out of this

world. Because it brought back "repeat performance,"
destruction and all.

As I mentioned earlier, there was nothing to sighting that
Moon as it glowed and moved along at first. In fact, this was
expected. It would travel along its path, and settle over the
western horizon to rise again the next day. But when it was
blacked-out unexpectedly that night, and there was no more
light that night (or that Moon) then the eyes grew suspicious.
What had exactly happened to it? Especially since this
sweeping motion had only changed the position of those two
clouds? And they were completely separate from that Moon?
Odd, how that happened. How watching how the clouds had
shifted in mid-air, and that the Moon had disappeared behind
them left only a cover of darkness. And nothing else; because
when that visual activity stopped, and the Moon was no
longer present, it looked as though there was a single dark
cloud that appeared in its place, which was the end result of
that wind (storm) which had come in announced.

That visual commotion, once it calmed itself, generated
that one big black cloud and no more movement for the eyes
to see. And that is what seemed to be odd to the eyes. They
thought that the Moon should still be behind it, since their
forward motion and that entire scene had disappeared. And
though it was completely dark outside (prior to this), now
with that huge dark cloud and its coverage, it kept the

Moon's light from penetrating any further into the darkness. The removal of this light also seemed to signal that the Moon had actually stopped too; as if to lay in wait behind this cover. But without that visual stimulation, it was also supposed to quiet the mind; but it had not. In fact, if nothing else that dark cloud and its coverage overly stimulated the mind, because without that light penetrating through that darkness, it made it seem like it was too dark outside. And that made the mind think there was more going on out there than there really was.

Stilled air though, is wonderful, is it not? But apparently not; at least not that night. When that Moon lay hidden behind that one large black cloud, it was thought that the Moon would reappear as it once was. And it was only a matter of time when it would reappear once more that night in its entirety. And the illusion would be uncovered. But there was no illusion to speak of, what was taking place in front of those eyes was in real time; the only "illusion" was that the mind had pre-determined the Moon that it should be sighted that night and more than likely in that same space. Only that too was a part of the disclosure. That larger cloud, when it had been swept away by an even stronger wind, not only uncovered that black space, but the fact that there was no Moon there in that specific place to see ever again. But that did not keep the mind from watching and hoping that the Moon would re-appear once more that night.

The reason for this anticipation had more to do with what one hoped to see before the Moon dipped below the horizon; and it wasn't the Moon itself per se one wished to see, but the whole entire picture once more. That is until the realization struck home: those two clouds which also added to her loveliness that night were no longer there. They had been swept away through the force of the wind. And now there was only that sound to deal with.

Although the light and the Moon had been removed from that point in space, there was still this sound resonating in that space instead. And why it did, seemed even more elusive than that blanket of darkness which had infiltrated that night air. These same night air particles were not just enriched with light, but they had sound emissions in them as well. So even though the light transmissions were being blocked by this one big black cloud, which had sequestered the Moon and her glow; there still were emissions coming forth out it: Signaling all was well. And how would we know that? Because of the silence; there was no sound to hear previously, and based on that we presumed that meant all was well. But once we learned that was not true, it became a matter of concern. In fact in all that quietude there actually was more to be feared than that noise and that resounding, boom. Because once one heard how it had been manufactured by the strength of those winds combining with those outer structures, then, not only did we see air, but now we could hear it. And know what it stood for.

The rushing of that wind not only caused that scene to disappear, it also made that concussion possible. When those air molecules burst, they made that sound. And that was caused by that wind as it rushed through a very condensed airspace. Which is why when it did, it was literally pushing at the sides of that space, forcing itself to go through it; which then forced what was there, i.e., the other air that was there to move up or to move down. And these movements literally cleared that night air, but also gave what was there virtually no other choice: move up, down, or die-out. Same as the light, right? No, not really. Because light waves do not react on us the same way that sounds do. Sounds reach us internally much faster than light. And why might that be?

When we hear, we are using a sub-system of our bodies, our auditory system. So when a baritone sound such as this boom enters our bodies through this sub-system, it not only is heard as a sound at the lower end of the decibel range, but it is also felt there too; it is felt deeper than other tones. And because of its tonality, it can be compared to other notes, lower or higher frequency ones. However, because this one was manufactured by Nature (and at night), it seemed different mainly due to the way it was received; on only one side of the head. Causing not just the three middle ear bones on that side to vibrate, it also seemed to cause the larger bones in the head to conduct this sound as well. Thus, not only was that ear receiving this sound, but so was the other; but not as loudly. Now imagine that? Our bone structure could hear this sound almost in the same manner as those three tiny little ones; only they transmitted this sound into the inner ear without any trouble.

These three tiny bones actually transmitted this sound wave to the inner ear system upon impact. After they received that sound, as it had traveled through the ear canal to the tympanic membrane, where the air itself was stopped; it was then transformed into an electrical signal. An impulse that could then be transmitted to the brain so it could be further discriminated, as either a very loud voice or as a very loud noise. But when that noise compelled us to pay attention to it (rather than what the eyes saw), then it was the ear and the direction in which that sound came from that drew one's attention away from the sight, directly to the sound and its environmental impact. This miraculous inner ear system was impacted in such a way that when that sound reverberated inside of it, it caused a different kind of impression. It literalized that sound in such a way that "danger" was the only assumption that one could make after hearing it. Nothing wrong with that. There is definitely a need to have some sounds be exactly what they are supposed to be, signals that warn us not to come near them, or to find shelter, or to listen to them more intently.

Fluidity

How could a sound reverberate in such a way that it could be understood to mean, danger, and nothing else? Was it meant to be that way? When the fluid in this inner-ear system was rocked or swayed, it sent a signal to a specific region of the brain to touch off other places within this inner system. So while it was sending out these signals, causing motion to be felt, another part of the brain was not even touched by it. Only one side of the head was affected by this sound, which is what made it a uni-lateral movement; but when it descended, there was a syncopation felt in the gut, it too felt the re-percussions of that sound. The stomach felt the topsy-turvy movement produced by that sound reverberating in that inner ear chamber. However, what this ear-stomach combination did not know was why they responded to the noise as they did. For the stomach to feel this upset, it had to have experienced a sense of nausea. Right? Otherwise, how would it know that it was being affected by this inner ear connection? And that this was the result of that sound, after it had traveled through this neural circuit.

This sound was quite powerful, but so was this inner-external connection. Because without one or the other, the body would not know what sound was like, or that it could travel virtually undetected until it hit a nerve. Then we knew sound frequencies, volume, and the rapidity of a wave. But why would it take a feeling of being ill in the stomach to solidify something invisible, such as this sound? And why would it need to travel to this internal system, the stomach?

Just like any other place in the body, there are nerve fibers which feel for us. Which is why when they are disturbed for no apparent reason (except that they have been touched by something which is either familiar or unfamiliar to them), they respond as they do. There is no thinking in them. They are our autonomic reflexes responding to being fired due to some type of stimulation. So in this instance, the sound had stimulated the ears and the stomach causing them to feel the ill effects of that sound as it reverberated through the body. Weird as that may seem. And then as they were "feeling" this neurologically, they kept emitting signals, internally; basically, keeping this nocturnal stimulation alive, till it too died down. And because the body is hard-wired in this manner, it could continue this type of emission sequence each and every time that the ear and its system felt queasy.

That night air seemed innocuous until it was made visible by that noise and the wave that it had made, which caused the stomach upset. And it was felt to be this way, because it was not seen as a vital source of aural stimulation; until it represented more than what is normally expected at that time of night or from that kind of air. At night we expect the air to be either silent, or filled with normal nocturnal vibrations (e.g., those crickets chirps or the leaves rustling), common sounds which fill the night. But to go from one extreme to the other? From silence to this really loud sound, especially that late at night? Seemed unnatural; especially since no sound should have accompanied that nocturnal vision as it was traversing that early morning night sky, and it should have remained soundless, until the early morning dawned. Then the expectation that the air would be filled with aural excitations was expected, but not during the nighttime.

At night the air's excitement is supposed to die-down. There are fewer emissions for it to transmit, because there are fewer manufacturers and receivers of them. At least that is the theory. However, when that airwave shook the night as it did, shaking everything that was still out there, the warm air and the silence; and then all it left in its wake was the dark and this sense of nothingness, then we knew the night air was shifting. It was turning over in its sleep. Ever hear of Night doing this? Turning over before the dawn lit up the sky?

Etching that night post its disappearance did not even come close to what it was like to be present and completely attentive to it, while it was displaying what it was capable of. It was quite an expressive scenery. So even when it was completed, it still transferred, registered what it was doing upon those three receptive senses: the ears, the eyes, and the stomach. Weird as that all seems. Yet had it not, would it have made the kind of impression that it did? But we cannot return to a non-agitated state, now can we? Once that impression was made internally, there was no looking back or returning to, to even consider. And unfortunately when that happened, i.e., our bodies had received that sight and that sound, it was too late. Partly this was due to our passive system; how our bodies are hard-wired to receive signals that activate it; but also it had to do with the interior aspects. Could the mind-brain attend to these signals just long enough for them to be felt? So they could be recognized for what they were, excitations. And then note the positive correlations between them, and not just hyper-focus on the negative? Was that at all possible?

One element that seemed to remain steady through all of this was the human. They had to be present to see the sight as it moved silently across the night sky. And then they had to be within the range of that sound and of the sight, for it to be seen as something more than just a silent movie. That sound actually re-animated it. Is that not weird? Yes, to say the least. Because seeing it in all that silence should have been enough visual and auditory information to document it; but, when that loud noise came from out of nowhere and re-stimulated this mental image, it no longer was just moving across the night sky without a sound. There was a sound bite attached to it now. And presumably if one human heard this sound and saw this sight, then no matter where it happened again (i.e., the near future or in a far distant land), then they too would know what it felt like to be impacted by this kind of perturbation. That is they would sense this image the same as I did. However, since no two people are hard-wired in the same manner, and their perspectives would be quite different than mine; then this would be impossible to test. Especially since, there would be no reality in which one could actually test this theory to even find out if one felt or thought the same about what I saw and heard that night. All we could depend on was "me" for that kind of information, and my retelling skills. Right? So then, replicating that exact moment in time became ruthless.

The only way that I knew how to exact that same image was to repeat myself. But to do so without going into a lot of non-sense or irrelevant literature, and so that meant discarding with quite a few of the details; even skimming over the most pertinent. And why might that be? Because of the contusion, and the commotion; these two seemed to cause the most con-fusion. So without them, then the simplicity of that one sighting would be easier to transmit onto these few pages. And one could do so in record time. That way one could get their true perspective in place before it too disappeared (which was quite similar to what had happened to that nocturnal image sans that sound). But once that sound was in place, it demarcated that panoramic image. Now it had two auditory components to it: a silent one, and a noisy one. These then further differentiated that image into two features: a silent one, which mainly had visual stimulations coursing through it; and an auditory one, which held the audition aspects. So then if one wanted to capture this entire panoramic scene in its entirety, one would not only have to watch as those scenes unfolded, but one would have to listen too. And then note the endings. But to do that simultaneously while also being charged with transcribing that nocturnal sight, seemed not only ludicrous, but questionable too.

Why would anyone in their right mind work on something such as writing verbatim what one was seeing taking place out there? And then once this was completed (or nearly so), turn it around and rework it night and day, just so one could be assured that what was being transcribed was copasetic with that nocturnal scene. Because not to rework it to this point, seemed detrimental. But it also seemed to elucidate the scene too. Making it as transparent as one possibly could.

One could not go back in time literally, but the more one reworked the past, the more one could bring forward what remained of it. And that was good. But one also needed to know what aspects from there, i.e., from the past (and not just this panoramic image) one really needed to hone in on. Because that helped Memoria, strengthened her; and that was extremely powerful too. This storage facility, not only held visuals but emotional content. Thoughts and feelings which had been secured too many different kinds of illustrations; and because they had been, they were also intra-related to the short-term. That is, one could virtually pull up what had just happened moments ago, without any trouble whatsoever; but the long-term memories, they took much longer to reconceive.

But this time differential was the key, was it not? If one could reconceive these short-term memories along with their emotions within a few seconds, then there was no need to re-see or re-feel them even with this visual. In fact, they were better sensed because they had not happened that long ago; however, these longer-term ones needed time (days) to resurface so they could be felt. And mainly that was due to how they had been penned. Their wordage is what caused them to need an image or some type of visual clue for the mind to hone in on so that they could be remembered with as much emotional content as could be expected. However, the audition (if it was directly given) did not need the visual or the image to incite its remembrance. It just needed to be practiced, orated even. And why might that be? Because of the oral-aural pattern and the physical nature that kind of signal reproduced; it was a recursive one.

Why was the aural aspect not dependent on the visual or the pictorial? And more importantly, why after hearing that sound that night, was there now a physical component to it? Because it had been insighted; no longer was this just an airwave with baritone qualities in it. Instead, it now held this other image to it: a mushroom cloud. This preternatural occurrence had been insighted before, earlier when I first mentioned how this loud sound vibrated, first reminding me of where I had first experienced it. At a jet show, where they performed aerobatic maneuvers which broke the sound barrier, causing windows to vibrate, and our ears to hear their roar. But since then, I no longer hear that sound in the same manner. In fact that is what is so dis-gusting about getting this signal from the environment and the wind's impact as it forced its way through that night. I no longer hear that sound in the same manner as I used to. Now I hear it differently, as a traumatic event that not only affected the ear and the head, but the entire sensate body; thus alarming the whole system. But was this not also mentioned as an after-effect? That once one was impacted by this peculiar sound systemically, it could go on resonating for hours, before it was no longer heard. Which was wonderful, especially if we no longer desired to hear it; but it was waiting while it was resonating that we could no longer tolerate.

Waiting without knowing how long it would take before this sound dissipated, was out of our hands. And rightfully so; because this allowed our bodies to do what it needed to do with this sound. And if it meant that our stomachs needed to feel queasy for a time, so be it. And if it also meant that we needed to listen to it internally a bit longer than we would have preferred (and not mask it), then we should. We should leave it to resonate interiorly until it no longer was felt. And then once it was gone, we then knew what it was like to hear that roar and rush of that wind, as a boom that sent the entire system into an alarm status. And though externally this signal only lasted for a matter of seconds, interiorly it resonated for hours, disturbing it; which was good to note. And why is that? Because now we knew what it must have been like to be in danger at one time, and to be barely conscious of it.

Why would a loud noise such as that boom that night disturb us so thoroughly? Unless, it held another scene in it; and as I already mentioned, it did. But it held this power in it too; as though without its presence in that scene, then we would not be attending to it or making any other associations to it other than what I have already described. True enough; because without it and the way that it resounded through us that night, and had continued to do so, there would be no need to continue to describe what it must have been like to see that cloud rise above the Earth's surface after that bomb was dropped without a sound. Besides without that sound would we even know there was such a thing as a sonic blast? Hard to know, unless we turn to Earth and listen to what she manufactured with our assistance, our weather patterns; then we might know what the Earth sounds like when she is "blowing." Now would that not be a novelty? The Earth literally making loud sounds with us captured inside of her biosphere. And what if, re-inventing that peculiar noise at that particular time of night was supposed to capture our ear? And our mind with a warning? Would that not be a hoot? And a quick reminder that the Earth could produce a note such as this, and we had better listen, or else. So was that what the Earth was trying to alert us to? That if we did not take care of the air and the environment, she would lose both? The air that surrounded us and those weird weather patterns that supposedly contributed to that sight and that sound being produced that night. So we had better be listening; because we may not have any air to speak of, or weather.

But was that not what those environmentalists were always warning us about too? So, why did the Earth that night need to appeal to us as well? Was there a collaboration of some type? And it took both to wake us up to the dangers of that sound-noise? Possibly. Let us suppose then that it was an orchestration between these humans and Mother Earth, and it was not necessarily the sound that was produced that disturbed us the most, but the remembrance of it and the manner in which it was repeated that night. Because it sounded like it was a storm brewing, and all one had to do was look out one's window and see it.

To see a storm warning in the dark, after having seen that beautiful image was more disturbing than not being aware of either. But what was even worse, was our part in it. We watched as it unfolded that night from a place of observation only. With no intentions of doing anything else, except report on what we were seeing; that was all. But then, once that sound broke through that night, and left what it did in its wake, then it became apparent that what was also taking place out there was quite unusual. It was not the usual wintertime storm or just a shift between night and day. There was something about how that image came together and then dissipated sans that sound.

There was more to this nighttime image then just the way in which that Moon moved through the night untouched by it all. In fact, she seemed to float through the night air undisturbed by what was taking place here on Earth. And since she had this capacity to wander the night sky unscathed, her disappearance that night also made me wonder about her. Why had she appeared that night "clothed" as she was? That was quite a mystery. But so was her abrupt disappearance that night. What had happened to make both of those nocturnal appearances so inviting? In the first scene she was bathed in a goldish-brown glow, traversing the early morning night sky with those two clouds in the lead. Then when they disappeared, apparently so had she; but they did not accomplish this all at once. As I mentioned earlier, the thinner wisp of a cloud was dispersed first. Which then left that larger cloud and her intact; quite a magnificent feat actually, since when that airstream moved that thin cloud aside as it did, it did so with nothing more than a puff of air (or so it seemed). But this wisp of cloud and its dematerializing was what startled the eyes, and though its lateral movement was just a curiosity at first, keeping our eyes watching it, it also signaled something else was taking place out there, and one could pay attention to its dispersal or simply choose not to. What do you mean one had a choice?

Well, one could watch how that airstream had moved that cloud and contemplate how that had come about; or one could watch what happened to the Moon and that larger cloud after that small cloud had been transversed. And then see how this affected the visual field. There was now more room to see the Moon almost in her fullest, and that larger, darker cumulus cloud as they both hung there in the northern hemisphere just above the horizon. But once that was duly noted, then that goldish-brown glow was amplified and one could see it and that darker cloud even better than before. You mean because that smallish cloud had been moved without a sound, and it had been dispersed by that movement alone, there was now more breathing space and air? Well that is one way to think about what happened in that one very slow and diametrically opposing movement. But one could also see this as cleared-out visual space which then showed the Moon's face all aglow even more so. But that Moon was not there alone. There was also this other cloud, larger than that other one hanging in the lower right-hand quadrant of that Moon's face. And it seemed to remain there too. That is until that gust of wind which also produced that noise burst in and dispelled both of them, or so it seemed. And I say this, because that wind not only moved that larger, darker and more condensed cloud to the middle, but in doing so, it also appeared to have blanketed that Moon and her glow. And because it was blacker outside now, it also seemed to be just a cover. There was still time for her to reappear once that blackness was dispersed. But that was the illusion, was it not?

The Moon was no longer behind that blanket and its coverage. But it looked to be so, if only for just a minute. Because, even though that big black cumulus cloud did appear to stop it, the Moon and the Earth kept right on rotating. And though we had hoped that the Moon would take a break from her activity that night, and reappear once that dark cover was dispersed, it was just not to be. Which was fine, but it was also disappointing too. And why might that be? Well, when that Moon stood out as she did that night, she appeared to be significantly different than an earlier sighting of her. And she was. She was not that cold, hard Moon once sighted by another, nor was she big, "bright" and white either. Her appearance there seemed out of character to these past representations of her. So then that could only mean one thing, this Moon and her shine were completely different than these past presentations; but also we desired to see her more than what had accompanied her that night: those two clouds. But since none of them were in return mode, except that wisp of a cloud, it seemed essential that their vision be documented for posterity's sake; if for no other reason than this. However, does it not also seem strange that a planetary vision would even need to be re-transcribed? That is taken from a verbatim observation of it as it unfolded that night, and then re-worked? And reworded several times just so the audience could also partake in its vision, which was? Ah, yes, the participation effect.

What was one supposed to do about that nocturnal vision, especially after it insisted it be seen from afar? Build a rocket ship and fly to the Moon and see why it happened to be that color that night rather than its usual color, white? But that was the irony, was it not? We could see this Moon and its variation of colors without having to build a rocket ship and travel in it to her space. In fact, we did not even have to move out of our chairs to see how it varied in color. All we had to do was look toward the sky at night and see what color that Moon was. But that was not all that attracted us to it, was it? Because we could also see how round or full it was; plus, whether or not it was even there. And with these added features, we could also discern the darkness, i.e., note how dark it was out there with or without her presence. Then we could use all of these to help us further. Such as, take what we knew about her up to this point, then take a real look out at the night sky and see what a huge difference she made that night. But why would we need to, if we have already seen her? Because looks can deceive us; as we know, but taking another good hard look at the Moon was impossible that night since she was being held behind that dark curtain. So how were we supposed to do a "reality-check" without being able to see her again?

Well that is a difficult question, especially in the realm of scientific inquiry. We would like to be able to concretize our first observations as gospel, but in the world of natural observations that is not likely to happen; plus it goes against every principle held in this kind of observational modality. We do not touch nor intervene, we only watch in silence. Eerie, huh? But it does not have to be felt in this manner, unless one looks at the Night as something to be feared, rather than welcomed. Then it is understandable why one may be in fear of it and what it displays. Or perhaps, it was not necessarily that the Night or that Moon and what it was displaying that night was what one feared the most. Instead of these, it was the anxiety brought on by that sound that cornered their passage. And that was what one was still concerned with; because it still resonated (despite our denying it was still present).

We thought that it had recoiled enough, but apparently not. Why would one want to know the feel of a sound?

Rather than just depending on one's hearing for this particular part of its quality? Because as I have already mentioned, sounds can be felt much easier in the body; and it is not just because of our ability to receive them two-way, sensorineurally and conductively, but also because we can "hear" them in our bodies as they electrify us, i.e., the sound pulsates and stimulates the brain. And when they do, they set off particular regions of it, sometimes it is just the temporal lobe that is being affected, but more often than not, it is also the occipital lobe too. At least it is for us bi-lateral learners. But here is what is so unusual about that kind of distinguishment. The brain does not know if it is a visual learner or an auditory one, all it knows is that it receives these signals, and then it is "charged." And, unfortunately for us all, it was being re-stimulated by this one peculiar sound again. Now why was that, especially since it was quashed just a moment ago? Because something must have made it reappear. But what could that be, if it was not that original sound, and it no longer was attached to either of those two scenes as was previously stated. Then what could it be? There was something about "hearing" and feeling it one's body that had disturbed it. Now is that not intriguing?

Vertigo

A sound is not typically enough to jangle the nerves, but in this instance, it was. And it did so in such a way that it sent a signal directly to the stomach and its contents. But it did not do so in a direct manner. It had disrupted the fluid within the vestibular system, and because it had this connection to the stomach, it also caused that area of the body to experience this signal, but not at the same time that it was expelled. So that meant there was a delay in the signal. In other words, one did not necessarily experience vertigo at the same exact moment one heard a sound or happened to watch something take place outside. In fact that was what was so strange about re-experiencing this signal, and now feeling this "illness." Only it was not an illness per se, but the body's normal reaction to being concussed.

The head had been concussed several times before this one night signal. And it had been by what were once considered normal volumes, transmissions of sounds. But now that these had been mitigated, there was less noise, i.e., less sounds. Or so it seemed. That night there was all this silence, and nothing to hear, but this. So when the head (ears) felt that nocturnal sound, it was concussed even more strongly; especially when that nocturnal sound seemed to come from out of nowhere, out of the dark and out into the open where it seemed to dispense with all of that silence. And it did. However, when this vestibular system had been startled, just as the ears and the head had been, it was too late for the mind-brain to note it. But they had. It was just that the eyes and the ears, along with their "visuals" had overwhelmed it; and the signals that this system had emitted seemed to have been lost. But they had not. In fact, in all that excitement this internal system had felt sick just as it was supposed to, only now it was registering in this mind-brain. Is that not strange? No, not really. The body knew what it was doing, absorbing all of these signals in silence that night. And it did so passively, because that is how our bodies are made: to absorb the impact of whatever happens to be manufactured or made out in nature. And mainly this is due to the way in which they are designed. They mainly are receptors, and then dispensers. And because they have this dual capacity, to receive and to dispense, they also have the capability to emit signals to various points within them. Is that not wonderful? Yes it is.

Except on this rare occasion, when that internal signal was masked and it should have been the first signal that we responded to, not the last one. But we cannot fault the way in which our bodies are hard-wired, can we? Not if we are supposed to leave them alone, and allow them to be as porous as they are. Yet, if we had not interceded and lessened the environmental noise, so we could hear twofold: silence and how quiet the night and the day could be, then we may not have re-registered there was a difference. But the irony in having done so? We could now discern this more recent concussion with former ones. Is that not wonderful too? No, it is not. Now why the change in heart?

Before, in that tiny transmission of sound, there not only was a loud factor but a deeper tone (as I noted earlier). Which, when it came through that cramped space, not only rattled the outside as it passed through, but it would have deafened the ear had it not been somewhat muffled by the body and by the houses and trees which stood in its path. Some of these outside structures acted as normal defenses, i.e., as wind barriers, preventing portions of the air from traveling through at its fullest; while other obstacles displaced it. Pushing it and changing it, even forcing it to be configured differently than its original shape; which as an invisible system, there really was not any true configuration for it to be, just this invisible force which blew from out of this one northeast direction and that it just happened to travel through at this time of night, bumping into whatever happened to be solid out there. And when it did, it was compressed and misshaped by those external structures; so that when it finally arrived in this open space, it literally burst out, emitting this intense sound. Strange how that sound was manufactured by that gush of wind hitting against all those solid structures till it erupted out in this clear space to be heard. But that was not all that was constructed in that turbulence.

The noise was only a part of that wind and its gusting ability. It also sent shock waves in its dispensing. That is as it moved throughout the environment that night; it was emitting forth powerful waves (bands) of air, even before this sound made its rare appearance, waking up our entire sub-system, i.e., the vestibular and inner ear system. Because even though it was awake and it was responding to that silence and then that sound as that nocturnal sight unfolded, it was not fully aware of the ramifications of having been "on" prior to hearing that sound as it came out of that darkness full-force.

All that we noted when this nocturnal sight was first encrypted was, either there was too much silence or not enough of it. Or, there was this sound and its startling effect. There was nothing to note from this vestibular system; that is, until one felt nausea or light-headed again. Then we knew we had been concussed not by this sight, but by that sound having come from out of nowhere. And it may have also had something to do with the side that this invisible force had actually come from, the northeast. But why should its direction and its full-on force cause this vestibular system to elicit a signal now? Especially since it had been buffered before? What do you mean buffered? Well, prior to that commotion, this vestibular system was at rest; not because it was not being impacted by that soundless night, it was. But it lay in this undisturbed state because it had not been put into motion, i.e., being rocked or swayed, until that silence was broken by that air streaming in as it did which caused it to be moved. Then it felt concussed, just as it should; because now its fluid had been disturbed. So what did that mean? Well, it meant that this inner-ear relationship had worked in syncopation with the unfolding of that nocturnal vision - but not through the eyes, through the ears. But even more importantly, through the bones as they had conducted that vibration virtually bypassing the ears; the strength of that vibration shook the head as I mentioned before, and that is what led to this fluid being disrupted.

The body had been co-constructed to interact with the environment, and this included what lay outside in the world beyond it. And since it was constructed in this manner, it also felt accumulations differently. That is, it could feel the weather as it moved in, e.g., feeling it deep within one's bones, arthritis. But it could also feel, sense other movements too. Such as, what it was like to be bent into a ball-like shape, and then tumbled forward in a rotating motion, i.e., somersaulted, and then note what that was like. Basically, the head felt dizzy and out of sorts, and the stomach "churned." And though one was no longer in this motion or bent in this ball-like shape, the body was still responding as if it still was. So even though the body was no longer contorted or in motion, the head was still reeling from this simple somersault. Now why might that be? Because of what was stored within it. There were all these various sub-signals still emitting their signals to the brain for it to detect, and to deal with. And since it was the place where all of these sensorineural signals came together, congesting it, it took time for it to decipher them as all these emissions were being "felt" simultaneously. And since some of these emissions were electrical, they appeared to reach the area they were supposed to and do so rather quickly. So then they could begin dissipating, but then there were these other signals which seemed to keep emitting their upheaval. And since they were, the head kept feeling like it was spinning, and this made the stomach feel nausea. And yet, one could do nothing but wait out these effects, right? And do so feeling as if this vertigo would never end. But it did eventually, which was a "blessing in disguise," I guess. What a way to conclude this, after having been through that kind of disruption.

It was not that this vestibular system's movement and the resulting vertigo symptoms were anything to "write home about." But they were. They made one feel ill, no doubt about it. However, just because they did, it did not mean that they had to be reported on at that moment (or even now).

Hard-wired as it was, the body (and now the mind), knew not only how to respond to this vestibular system's "upset" but also what to do to keep it from ever feeling light-headed or nauseated again: Avoid the behavior. That was the easiest solution, after those jangled nerves finally quieted down. Plus, this solution made common sense. Do not engage in activities where a concussion could re-occur, such as tumbling or twirling (or unfurling this nocturnal scene), because these will upset that system after it had righted.

After that fluid in the vestibular system resonated, and those jangled nerves were deciphered by the mind, then all that remained was avoidance. How did one avoid disturbing that system? By not engaging in those activities which caused it to feel out of kilter; seemed logical enough, and even easier to follow since one now knew what tumbling and unfurling that night vision did to oneself. It made it feel out of focus and ungrounded (strange as that may seem). But how could that be? How could a physical activity concuss the mind and the body? Especially since watching, listening, and then transcribing that vision was considered a passive activity, while the other was just a simple motoric endeavor? And yet, both concussed the brain in the same manner. Was there something wrong with it? And that was why it responded similarly to these two, as though it had been injured? But it had.

When this internal system responded as though it had been concussed, it was not just the head and the body that had received it that way. It was also the outside: it too felt the concussion of that wind and that sound, which is why it seemed so abnormally excited that night. When those airwaves shocked this system, all of these elements were responding in kind to what had taken place in the environment. It was being infused with all of these signals: light ones, sound ones, even "nothing" ones. Which seemed odd; these kinds of excitations did not typically take place at night. And therefore, when they did, they seemed abnormal. There were too many vibrations and reverberations happening all at once for this system to abreact to. As if any of those external structures could respond emotionally to these vibrations and the resounding of them, or even know what the appearance of that nocturnal sight and that sound first meant to us. Or even cared. But is that not what we desired in a parallel system? For it and us to feel in-synch with each other, so that we could all experience those vibrations and reverberations in the moment in which they were presented. And since that is what seemed to be desired the most, then it was quite possible that one could be in-synch or in a parallel process with this system. And think nothing of it. One just "felt" simultaneously; that was all.

As I mentioned earlier, the eyes had watched that shift take place, but they were not the only ones "involved" in this system. The ears were also involved. But because they were, they also seemed overwhelmed by it all (and rightfully so). They were after all, only our receivers. And so it was not up to them to unscramble all of that stimulation; only to gather it and transmit it to the brain. And they had, just as they were pre-programmed to do. However, although they functioned exactly as they were supposed to, it did not mean it was up to them to decipher what they had collected and transmitted; that was supposed to be the brain's duty. It was supposed to be the place where all of that stimulation went so it could to be "read" while being distributed to the right area of the brain for storage. But that did not mean that once it arrived there, it did not get over-loaded with these stimulations. Because it did; but that was good for it, because then it was being stretched beyond its usual capacity. But that created something that was new to it, inner tension. Tension that was not there before; because before that night vision entered its realm, it basically had been able to deal with those physical sensations, nothing to it. But now that it had this nocturnal image and those others in its store, it too was filled with cryptographs, i.e., secret messages which it could choose to decipher or decode at random.

Is that not why there are times when visions, e.g., auditory and visual ones, just happen? And they appear to come to us, from out of nowhere. But now that we know they are manufactured from this one area, i.e., the brain, it should also be quite gratifying to know that they are made here, and not somewhere else. Because if they were, we might think (or hear) these intrusions in our thoughts as hallucinations; and that would completely discredit them. And why might that be? Because, even though this hard-wired system is abreacting to being over-loaded, and it emits, it does not disqualify the visions; although they are no longer present. They were there once before and that was all that mattered to the mind. In fact, when that wind brought that beautiful picture onto the western horizon, holding it there just long enough for it to be sighted, it was also enough for the eyes to insight it. And for the ear to hear the silence that had accompanied it; and then together, for them to be startled when that nor'easter blew in with all of its might and virtually destroyed that nocturnal vision. Because once it did that, then it became even more difficult to redesign it by this visual means only. Which meant that it had to be cemented in the back of one's mind, i.e., occipital lobe, or it would be lost forever, or so it seemed.

Remember when they nor'easter blew in from the north, it not only shifted the air that night, and dispensed with what was there, it also left this cold, darker air in its place. And when it did, it also looked like there was no light to see by; which was true. The Moon had continued on, and so what light that it brought into that airspace was also long gone. Which made that night air seem even darker, even more condensed; than seemed necessary. However, how was one to know what was necessary for that Moon to shine that night? Well, we knew. It needed the Sun and its solar rays. And it needed to be centered in a certain direction for us to see its fullness, and its glow; otherwise, it would have looked like any other Moon in all of its glory. Right? Wrong, and dead wrong. That Moon's glow that night was spectacular. Its discoloration was like toffee, smooth and milky-brown and edible too; which was another reason why seeing it there, made me desire her more than their re-assemblance. She was beautiful, and it did not matter if those two clouds reappeared that night with her; all I wanted to see was her again. But that did not happen either. All that meant, though, was that how the environment had co-constructed that image that night was not going to repeat itself, ever. And that was fine. But that did not mean that the mind had not copied it while it was in this motion-no motion state. It had. And it had recopied this image several times over, before re-producing it in this static state. But why would want to? Especially after all of that upheaval? Good question. What drove one to replicate what was no longer there? A need, perhaps? Yes, I would say that was a pretty good guess. But what that need was? Well that depended on the individual, right? Yes and no.

Some nighttime events are easier to describe than others. And also easier to record and transcribe, even to oneself. Strange as that may seem. But is it really that strange? Especially now that we know a bit more about denial and how it works to suppress some of our own knowledge, and it does so as a well-honed defense.

Now why would I say that?

Semi-permeable Biospheres

First impressions, as most of us know, may lead us into not thinking. In fact, we economize and take what we see literally at face value. And then based on this first look and this unique ability to summarize, we gather what we see is basically the truth. But this first impression and our economic ability can be deceitful. Not on purpose, mind you. It just happens to be the way in which we see and understand the world at first. In that very first gathering look we are laying a foundation, a mark, on which to base all future understandings. So within those first few milliseconds (as we are gathering this visual world, and economizing it in the process); we miss some crucial elements. Such as, what attracted us to look? The physical maturity of the mechanism, which had detected the external movement; and then from there, other elements, colors, shades, shapes and sizes; and as this visual field accumulated these, it drew upon this visual information to decode what it was seeing out there currently. So in this instance, there was a big round Moon and it was glowing with that toffee color. And there were also these two white clouds moving along with it. And they all were traversing across the night sky in-synch. However, as I have previously mentioned that was not all that was captured in that visual sight. There was also the auditory component. First, there literally was no sound, and then there was. Which meant the ears recognized this as silence, and then when this sound was produced, it shocked them into listening to determine what that noise was, and it was a boom! A loud enough sound that it shook the ears out of their revelry, and into active listening, even though they were already in this active state. In other words, though the eyes can close and also shut-out anymore visual stimulation from entering, the ears do not have this capacity. They do not even have the capability to close once they are opened, which means they are constantly on and are never rested. But they are when there is complete and unadulterated silence. Then they know the distinction; however, "hearing" is not the only part of this auditory system. As I have already mentioned, when the vestibular system is also stimulated by sound, it is also disrupted and hears this sound as a function of being disturbed. That is, initially it was lying in a steady state, unaffected by the silence. And, it remained in this position unmoved by the visual component. But then this sound came from out of nowhere, and disrupted it. Sending shocked waves throughout it. This then resulted in the eyes losing their focus, and the head to reel, and the stomach to feel ill; all because this sound resonated loudly. Not just outside, where it rattled the structures as it passed through it; but inside too. But for a signal to have that much strength initially? That seemed abnormal, and it was.

It was abnormally loud because of what preceded it: nothing but silent air. As it moved across the northern hemisphere with nothing but visuals held within it, there was nothing for the ears or this vestibular system to detect, but this noiseless night. Which was wonderful; till that night air was cleaved by that sound and that removed that silent motion. But it also served as a solidifier, i.e., it literally acted as end to that panoramic view. That as the night wore on, there would be more to pay attention to, but there was not. In fact, after that sound resounded, and that airstream continued to move through, colder and darker, there literally was nothing else to pay attention to; only the leftover residuals. The feeling of this vibration initially, and the "ill-effect" that it had on the vestibular system, and the other two senses, the ears and the eyes; and as I mentioned, they too were affected by this over-loaded sound wave as it reverberated through that cramped space. In other words, these two sensing organs and the vestibular one went unscathed until they were startled awake by that very loud sound, which alarmed them. Because it was not meant to be there in that really lovely silent picture as it unfolded that night in silence. But once it made its appearance, there was very little one could do but react to it in silence. So one did. One absorbed that sound, and also the impact that it had on those exterior elements: one heard the rattling of the windows as they vibrated from that gust of wind coming through; and one felt the temperature dropping as it brought this coldness with it; and lastly, note how there was nothing left out there, but this darkness. And how it seemed to lay in wait (or at least I did) thinking that this scene too would change, but it had not. In fact that was what was so gratifying about projection, one could send all of these thoughts, feelings, and assumptions into this perfectly cleared out night sky, hoping that what was seen previously, would reappear there: The Moon in all its eloquence. That is the realist in me, you know.

The ability to frame a first impression in this manner, though, allowed for it to be scrutinized more thoroughly. Especially in the light of day; because after having watched it unfold as I did during that night, noting how it transversed the night sky unfettered, till it bumped into this northeast wind, and then this sound, it seemed to be nothing but a beautiful image, unmarred. But then when it was blocked by this invisible wall, and seemed to just hang there, it also seemed to be waiting. Now is that not visually strange, especially in terms of a first impression? When a first impression is not supposed to be stuck, hanging in mid-air supposedly. But it can be. Now that is weird! Yes, it is.

How can a first impression which seems to be ambling across the northern night sky, unhampered, move into an invisible wall and then just seemingly, hang there? Well, there are plenty of rational explanations. But that night when there was this transmission, all that was visible in that darkness was that beautiful image and its symmetry. It looked like it fit into all of that darkness. And it did. However, when it bumped into this mysterious wall, i.e., this invisible force field, it also seemed to just hang there, in silence. While this airstream came through it, and moved that wispy cloud aside, disturbing the visual field; but also its silence.

That is the eyes were actually in slumber while they were captivated by that first sight. And would have continued to be, had it not been for that air being disturbed as it was; dislocating them from this state of mind. Strange as that may seem now, since the need to watch that scene unfold while also transcribing it verbatim seemed so intense; and that this state of mind needed to be captured too. So that nothing would be missed. But when there was this new movement, they were awakened from that strange staring state, and into this new reality. Which then caused them to be startled out of their trance-like transmission state, and into action; as if what they were seeing and intently honed in on was not enough. Now one had to watch what was now taking place outside. As if that new movement commanded it: Pay attention to this night vision because it is going through its own revision. And it is doing so apparently, all on its very own. And it was (from a naturalist's point of view).

Here was this Moon and these two clouds, which had apparently been blocked by an invisible force, forcing them to remain on the horizon. And then in enters this wind unexpectedly, blowing through this entire scene. And when it did, it moved that thin, wisp of a cloud to the center. But here it becomes murky, and not as well detailed. While they were being held there in this lateral space by this invisible force, it also seemed like they were being shielded, but only in one direction. And this gave one the illusion that this side of the shield could not be penetrated. So when that wind came in from that direction, i.e., from the west, and moved only a part of that picture to one side, to the center of that moonscape. It was seen as an intruder. The wind had entered that biosphere from the west, which was also where this shield effect had also arisen. And because of this, it also seemed to change the very idea that there was a solid wall on which this image could bank; which was odd, since it seemed to stop the all-in-one motion that had appealed to the eyes. However, when that wind entered from the opposite direction in which that notion had appeared, it completely blew it away, i.e., think nothing of it. And that is just what one did: thought nothing. This was quite refreshing. Especially since this area of the mind desired nothing more than "no more thought." And the permission too, to give it no more thought. Because then it meant, *one did not have to.* And when that happened, i.e., when that interpretation was held to be true, then one literally did not have to think any more. All one had to do was return to what they were doing before that wall was hit, and before that wind came through that impenetrable wall, disrupting that nocturnal vision.

There, unfortunately, was no going back to that "once before" or "once again state" once the eyes had beheld that vision, and the disruption. Because once they had seen what had taken place out there, and had sensated those motions they were impacted through and through. Saturated; which was good news for those of us who truly believe in the immersion principle. And what it can do to us. Change our minds, and do so in the immediacy. And why might that be? Well, once that air had cleared, and all that remained there was this murkiness, then it seemed too late to do anything about that dirtied air; but wait for it too to disappear. But it did not. In fact, it almost seemed to add a layer of its own to this panoramic vision, a thin layer of dust perhaps, but it was a layer nonetheless.

This dustbowl effect kept one's eyes mesmerized to it, waiting for it to settle. And just like that loud sound that had disturbed that silent picture, it too seemed to need time for it to register; but also for that night air to clear itself out of that space, so that what remained there could be readily seen: the Moon and that heavier cloud by its side. And additionally, this emptied space giving it a depth that had not been there before since it was originally sensated "flat." But how could a decompensation such as this, bring both clarity and substance to a natural observation? Especially when what it made it that way, was air? And the way in which the Earth and the environment moved, which caused that disruption that night.

Our ability to assess a situation rather quickly and then to make a first determination based on what is presented to us then and there is normal and it is abnormal. In fact, because we have this unique ability to perceive light years as though they happen right there in the moment, is also a deceit. Not an intentional one, mind you; but it is one nonetheless. Yet for us to admit this, seems self-serving; and it is. We humans need an escape mechanism. And it just happens that there are many out there to choose from. So some of us may choose watch and observe what takes place out there in outer space, others may listen to it too. Is that not wonderful that we can all be so intent on what happens there, rather than listening and observing what is taking place closer to home? Yet, had we not listened and learned about what took place here on Earth first, and then made the necessary adjustments so that they could be transferred what lay outside of us, we may not have known about what these airwaves were transmitting, light; but also sound. But in all that murkiness, there were dust particles or dirt, and some other substances which had clouded it; muting its ability to transmit clearly. But it did not remain this way.

Remember after that nor'easter blew through causing that ear-splitting sound? And it rattled not only those external structures, the houses and the trees, but the windows too? And because they too were impacted by this wind, they made that noise seem louder, amplifying it. But the element that was most impaired by this account was the human who just happened to be awake and present to it, when it appeared (and then disappeared), just like that; no warning whatsoever, except post-impact. Yet the residual of that air being disturbed, kept on resounding. So what did that mean to us today, months later when its transmission no longer seemed to matter? Nothing, right? Because only one human being was impacted by that sight and that sound and their transmissions, so it really did not matter if they had; what seemed to matter the most was that what had been transmitted that night had reached its final destination. Which was? Well, we may never know. We can summarize the sight and sound signals had been sent, received, and registered. And were now being transcribed verbatim from memory and reference to what had been sighted and heard.

But we also know this that sight and that sound transmission were long gone. And what remained, the externalization: the remembrance of that first sight and that sound as they co-constructed that panoramic view; and the re-citing of it over and over and over again, while documenting it on the inside. And that is what made the recursive cycle, excitations experienced on that first night which also co-existed with the elicitations. And in this cycle, something of value, which apparently had not been there before, time. This allowed for the following: the first sighting of it to re-register, and for those three physical internal structures to resonate as long as they needed to it and the resonation. But these all had a stopping and a starting point, did they not?

First, the ears only had a set range of tones and frequencies for them to pick-up sound and differentiate these even further by volume. They could also detect sound's presence, i.e., it should either be there or it should not. Secondly, the eyes could only gather so much material (i.e., what was presently there in the immediacy). Thirdly, the vestibular system had been hard-wired so that its range of motion was harder to detect. That is, it could remain untouched, i.e., in a steady-state no matter how the head and the body were positioned, till they rose up or turned too quickly, then it was unsettled. Alerting us to this fact and to this system's presence; otherwise, when we felt the ill-effects of it, we may not have known it had these two positions. Or that it could be affected by sound and that it could be concussed in this way, by a simple transmission.

Remember when that blast of night air with that sound encapsulated in it came through? And in it was nothing but air, this sound, and this rushed sensation? And then once it blew through that space with these elements in it, it left in its wake its residuals: the baritone quality and its loudness, vacated air, and this cold sensation. All of which had been detected from memory, but also by the actual figure, i.e., what had actually taken place as that sound wave (wind, actually) traveled through that airspace.

Disrupting what was already there; and that was what was already taking place in front of the eyes as they sat there mesmerized, looking at the environment as it unfolded that night. But was that not wonderful? Yes, it was. Because as they watched and recorded what was taking place in all of this visual space, they were just doing exactly as they were pre-programmed to do: sit there and record what they observed. But once that sound system went through and disrupted them, the eyes were even made more nocturnally aware than they once had been. Which was odd; since the eyes seemed to be hyper-focused on that sight initially; and they were, truth be told. But, now they were informed differently. Once they were shook awake by those few residuals, they could see into that darkness. And gather there were no more light signals for the eyes to capture that night, except there were these new ones. But were they really? Once that night air was cleared of that slow motion picture, and there was nothing left to see except this cleared out air, then the eyes should have been "thrilled," and they were. Because that reactivated them, to look into that light (which was actually the dark), and see what made it that way. There no longer was the Moon and her light, which was actually just a reflection of the Sun as it cast its solar rays out into space, where they happened to be received at an angle that could then be reflected back to Earth, so that we could see her up there in our atmosphere. Is that not the most perfect transmission? Yes it was.

Self-reflection Revalued

The mind is so strange, is it not? Yes it is. But it was also this that caused the mind to seize for just a moment to recognize this too. Was it agreeing too readily to this simply-ed asked question? If so, then, either it had been self-taught to do so, or it knew more than it acknowledged when it answered it so readily. Either way, it had been asked and it had been answered; now we were stuck with this rhetorical equation. So, what in that simple opening equation had seized it so that it could make a rapid review, and then know that it was on the right trail? The term "strange" had. But why should that simple word used in that construction cause it to realize itself? Is that not weird? Yes, it is.

It was, after all, just a self-generated vehicle, a literary device that invoked one to answer without much thought given to the question or how it was constructed. But the word that was used within its construction, strange, was what alerted us to the way in which the mind massaged itself into playing with itself. It was, believe it or not, one of those words that once it was constructed in this rhetorical device held its power to entice the mind into its own little game. To play with this word or the construction of it; so for example, it was only seven letters. And they happened to be sequenced from left to right so that they made sense to us horizontally, i.e., we recognized this word immediately for what it stood for. But it was also because we had self-taught ourselves to read, to catch the literal meaning of a word, as a whole word initially. But then when it was constructed in this more complex design, as a rhetorical question, asked and answered by me then it became negatively connoted.

Why was that though? Was this because the way in which it was phrased in a linguistic tool that could be answered in the immediacy (and positively) that the word itself grew in strength, but also in this direction too? Yes! This then caused the mind to think about what it was asking itself: Was it really that strange? And that is why it was so

easy to acknowledge that it was this way? Or, was it because
the word that was used, strange itself, which gravitated the
mind to think of itself in this manner? Or, was it possible that
as the word gained in favoritism, i.e., a word, it grew in the
negative direction rather than in the positive? And that is
why it was so firmly entrenched in the psyche as a criticism,
which also made it quite easy to answer that it was so. But
that was not all. The word itself had been judged
appropriately. It was a true statement about the mind, and
what it contained within it was of a private nature. And yet,
were we not supposed to know everything about this simple
word, and what it held in it? And why it pertained to opening
up one's mind to what was in it. And that was all this
negativity. Really? Really.

Naming the mind "strange" also lead to it filling with
similarly named objects. Some of which cast it into thinking
what it truly meant by this word. For example, hearing the
crickets chirp late at night, and then not hearing them ever
again. That would be strange, would it not? But so would
listening contently to the leaves rustle while the winds
passed through them, and not thinking much about it. And
one should. Because without the leaves and the noise they
made when the wind passed through them, then we would
not know the wind made noise or that leaves could rustle. Or
that without either the leaves or the wind and their

movement, there would only be silence. Silence, though, was not that strange initially. In fact, it was something which we had been accustomed to, even desired. But without the leaves present, so that they could be encountered by the wind, there would not be any movement or visual noise acquainted to them. That is correct. Yet, how would we know that the wind came through as it did that night? Without seeing the leaves on the trees to alert the eyes that there was a wind present? And there was not. There were not any leaves on the trees that night. However, there was this visual noise and there was also this quiet accompanying it. Which was to be expected; this visual field was full, but it was also empty of sound. As it was supposed to be; but this made it seem as if the wind could whip through leaving no noise behind it or for us to see. And that also was true. But when we expect to see something in that cleared out, open space, e.g., leaves, and they are not there as expected; our mind begins to play tricks on us. It fills in this empty space for us. And it does this with what it already knows should be there, out in all that darkness: Movement and no movement. Right? Yes.

So then, why would it disturb us when there is all this opened space? Is it because it is too quiet (to the eyes) and therefore, it needs this area to be refilled? And that is why the mind begins to draw from memory what was once there, or should be, or had not been there for a very, very, very long time. But is that not also moving us into unfamiliar territory, i.e., into perception, and how the eyes can be deceived before they actually know what they are receiving. And therefore, without actually meaning to, turn right around, and deceive us? Yes. Right again. But how could that be? If our mind receives what it is supposed to, and it does so with our eyes, then how could it then receive these transmissions correctly and then turn them into deceitful visions? Was there something in their transmissions that were penetrating more than just one's optical eye? Yes, and that was how they were perceived. But perception also meant being able to perceive the whole at once, and know that when one did one could also splice it and dice into many bits and pieces literally. And then store it that way too.

Is that not weird that this unique human ability allows for us to bring in an entire visual, one that literally has a beginning and end, which can then be scrutinized, analyzed, even left whole, i.e., untouched for many a century. Perception can do this for us. But when it does this, holds an image in place without a middle apparently, it also loses its continuity. And why might that be? Because it literally likes to tie everything into neat little bundles; although as a function of the mind and its cognitive capacity, it is supposed to receive everything complete; and it does not matter if there is a set beginning or end (or even a middle) when one is literally in this mindset. Is that not strange? Yes it is.

Yet, all one had to do was understand that light pulsated and radiated outward and that when it did, it traveled in light years, so by the time those few emissions reached us, they could be seen in their entirety; and they were. But then we had to label these based on how our minds actually perceived. Did they see all in one picture, or did they need assistance to see it all? And if so, how was one to know which was which without performing a little test on our self? But was it not dangerous to do so? To test one's mind? Well, according this "lit" review, it was very, very hazardous to do so; especially to one's eyes. Now, why might that be so?

Solar rays burn night and day. And in the emissions there are hard chemical reactions converting themselves into gases and light, which also contain heat. But, without travelling to the Sun to know this? That would be strange to know, would it not? Yes it would. And why might that be? Because, for one we already know that the rays of the Sun literally burn 24-hours a day and that while they do, they are hot emissions. And to go anywhere near those, just for investigative purposes, literally lead to one's death. But to cells bursting inside of themselves too? Yes. That would not paint a very pretty picture now would it? No, it would not. But those two views also depended on whether or not one was thinking in terms of what one was actually doing such as flying too close to the Sun and literally beginning the melting process, while simultaneously realizing one had failed to reach it. But was that not a warning to us too? Yes, it was. And we had better heed it too. And why was that? Because to save a life depended on us knowing this, did it not? Yes, indeed it did. But also how one thought in complete pictures, too.

One thought in pictures? And in complete ones? Yes and apparently most of us do. There are a few exceptions of course who think in terms of whole words (images) that look like representations of art. And they are. But do they hold the same meaning to everyone? Well, as art objects they may; but that is up to the individual to interpret. Is it not? Yes it is. But in terms of memories and storage and whether one learned these as a whole? That too depended on the individual, did it not? Yes, it did. But is that not also a part of our perceptual field too? That we know that how one learns these or remembers them as wholes or as parts also informs how well one can contain a memory in its complete state.

Words, though, were words were they not? And they could stand alone as artistic components could. But what they represented to us, could not. They became insults to us whether we were aware of it or not. And that was not to be tolerated. In fact, those were fightin' words, and the image they entailed, a war-torn human relationship; one that one could not wait to get rid of or out of. But how could that be? With just words? How would one know they were insulting? Without knowing their intent? And how did one also know they had wanted to leave, without knowing more about the circumstances? Or that one wanted to get rid of "something" and they only knew how by fighting or inciting a war-torn image? Now does that not sound familiar? No, yes, sort of; this, again, is good for us to know. Now why might that be?

To grasp the whole effect before it was so named was also quite important to know. And why might that be? Well, because, not to know why perpetuated a disbelief; but apparently, a misunderstanding too. And that was that one could grasp war-torn structures rather quickly because one had been immersed in these one's entire life. But that would also mean then that one understood what it meant to hold an object in one's hand, as if it truly existed there; and it did. However, truly knowing that it did? Well that took supposition. Is that not strange for me to say so here? No, probably not. Now why might that be? Because, who in one's right mind would want to be engaged or be re-engaged in a war-torn system? Especially when most of us prefer not to think about our systems as torn apart in the first place? When in fact they were, but we refused to see them this way.

Now, why might that be, especially when we were just discussing "wholeness"?

Wholeness, though, as we were just discussing held to its own connotation. In fact it became a popularized term, one that had a theory and a philosophy already attached to it. Gestalt, simply put is, "a structure, configuration, or pattern of physical, biological, or psychological phenomena so integrated as to constitute a functional unit with properties not derivable by summation of its parts." This idea and the philosophy held within it just about ruined every thought I had or held on this definition. Is that not weird for me to re-instate here? Yes it is; but not as much as one would think. Now, why might that be so? Especially when one is only in one's conscious mind "talking"? But talking to oneself was normal, was it not? Yes, it was. And one thought so for a very long time; that is, until one felt morally obligated to, to talk to one's self. Now is that not weird? Yes, it is. If one was supposed to talk to oneself, as one was taught to, then how was one supposed to know this was normal? Because everybody was self-talking, right? And everybody was taught to do so appropriately, right? But to feel morally obligated to? And to know that is exactly what one was supposed to feel, morally obligated to talk to one self every now and again? Yes. Because if one chose not too? They would get all teary-eyed, and infuriated; even emasculated. But why might that be? Because, believe it or not, this too was an awkward subject to discuss in this day and time. Now is that not strange for me to say now? Especially when we are so modern in our thinking? When in fact, we are not; and thankfully so, because to develop a moral conscience one had to have a conscience first, did they not? Yes they did. But that too was too weird to even think or to even ponder especially in this day and age. Now why might that be? Well, because self-talk was supposed to mean reasoning within, and to do so consciously; and to do so without blunders or obstructions. But then we would not be laying our hearts out like an open book, now would we? No, we would not. And why might that be? Because to do so, meant one was psychologically-impaired or in peril of losing one's mind. But to admit freely that one was laying their heart out like an open book? Really? And to do so freely? Meant your mind was elsewhere, was it not? Yes, it was. And where was it? Why on that Full moon as I had seen it that night! And kept revisiting it, because what I saw there that night kept returning in its entirety, even now. Day-dreaming, huh? Yeah, well, you know, sometimes we need to now and again. Really? Really.

Why would an image Earth-produced continue to germinate feelings and thoughts? Well, typically when we think about an image in its entirety, we are also inter-relating to it as a visual aide. That part of our system that is hard-wired to look at the physical space in present time, observe it, and then make random judgments based on its appearance, and also decisions based on what is seen there in that space. Imagine that? Our minds are pre-wired to take snapshots with our eyes quickly, and then recognize what they had captured were our first impressions. And in them were all these "objects," things which apparently needed to be explained. But to whom? If one already knew these were images, and one already knew these were also snapshots of one's environment? Then to whom was one supposed to discuss these things with? Internally, ourselves. But externally? Who were we supposed to talk to or with about what we saw, or wish we had never seen? Somebody, right? Yes. And if we could not locate someone on the outside right away, then we needed to do something. Did we not? Yes. Otherwise, we would just burst with all of this information if we did not have someone to share it with. And we needed apparently to share this rather quickly, or else lose what we had just acquired. Or, what we had just seen. And we could not wait to write or etch it because here was all this excitement going on inside of one's self. And it just had to be re-recorded. Especially when retention was thought to be at one time, "a two-way street," as it still is today. But in what context do we mean? Do we mean as far as being able to retain what one knew or grasped in the immediacy? Or, do we actually mean retaining enough of what one just learned so one could conversate with some intelligence? Or, perhaps we did not care what the other knew, just that we needed to relay something as quickly as we could. And if that took writing something down on whatever happened to be handy, a stone, it was a memory worth retaining.

Appearances were important to us were they not? Yes, they were. But do we not reach a certain point in our lives when appearances are supposed to not matter to us? Yes, we do. So why do they now? Why does this affect us, especially when we had reached a stage or an age where neither appearances nor what they stood for, bothered us? Because, it gave us a sense of tranquility to know that we no longer needed to pay any attention to either of these. Was that not freeing us of what had encumbered us too? Yes, it was. But how so? How was it possible not to remember our appearances, but also not to give a hoot about them either? Seemed really strange, even to the extreme not to think about this, did it not? Yes, it did. But it also helped us to recognize this too. And that was supposed to suffice for the moment, which it did. But then as we grew more aware of our outer selves, we also grew disgruntled with these exterior shells. Now, why might that be? Had we missed something earlier? Or completely overlooked it intentionally; because it no longer mattered to us. But to someone else it did. And as we know that is where "shadows" and dark figures lurked in the dark, waiting to lure us away or even scare us into not confronting our worse fears and those were, US!

Funny, though, when we began to think about "us" in the normal sense of this term, we forgot what it truly stood for, foe. Strange how that came around again, is it not? No, not if one was truly aware of this. Then it would not be that strange to reconsider ourselves as foe now and again. Now would it? No, it would not. But each time that one did, one literally got closer to home, did we not? Yes, we did. But why might that be? Why not move into this subject right off the bat? Well to do so, meant certain destruction. But of what, pray tell? Our former relationships with ourselves. But was that not also a part of the package? That each time that we neared a part of us, it was lethal to us. Now why might that be? Because, when we neared a part of ourselves it was supposed to alert us to: time for a change and a drastic one. Now why would change be considered in this negative light? Especially when on the outside, we do not mind a little change now and again? In fact, some of us desire this change even more so. Huh, imagine that?

When we begin to think of change, though in terms of reality, one's integrity, or even one's reputation, then change was harder to think about. Let alone implement. Maybe that is why it is dreaded deep down inside? Maybe. But, when it came to seeing how our species had changed? That was not seen as a negative at all. In fact, this was so positively seen, it was difficult not to. But how could one verify this change without some kind of device, such as looking out one's windows toward the environment, and seeing this for certain.

The Quneitra Artifact A flat cortex plate (7.2 cm) incised with four nested semicircles and surrounding vertical lines, Levantine Middle Paleolithic, ca. 54, 000 B.P. (Marshack, 1996).

What one thought they saw here, in this inset was not what was originally insighted was it? No, it was not. Now, why might that be? Well, as I mentioned before looking at this artifact or even out one's windows perception does not guarantee accuracy, unless one was the primary observer.

Then one could be fairly certain, if not completely accurate that what one saw was an exact replication of an Earth-produced image. And it needed to be documented or etched in stone, just because it stirred one to do so. Now imagine that? But how could that be so, when we tend to think that Modern Man knew more about beauty than their prehistoric ancestors? But that is where we messed up. Who did? Who missed that this part of ourselves was muy importante, and caused such a riff between us? Scientists, perhaps? Or just that it takes years upon years to grasp what this truly was. An artifact that needed to be unearthed first, then for another mortal to happen upon it, and discover that it was a rainbow and not a tunnel or even an entrance into a cave seen from its interior. This crude etching carved in stone was one of the earliest forms of communication. And not till now, a rudimentary documentation of nature and what had taken place way back then. Is that not something to behold? Yes, it is. But even more importantly, this stone document pre-exited before writing, yet it still contained the same motoric movements; ones that elicited the hand to move more than once, and the brain to know that it already had this capability inside of it. In fact, to get this etching into this stone, one had to repeat, repeat, and repeat these same fine-gross motor movements several times just to carve this picture into the first piece of paper. And yet to be able to do that, meant sitting for hours alone rehearsing, what they had captured in their mind in that moment, and had to repeat in that piece of stone. And today we liken this to sitting for hours in solitary play, crafting.

This very simple psychological step was also supposed to prepare us to move into another kind of cognition, i.e., holding two thoughts simultaneously. No intermixing here, just two thought transmissions holding steady as one worked to understand both simultaneously. Is that not how our minds and our brains were first thought to be constructed? That we could hold two thoughts all at the same time, and still work on what was right in front of us. And not think in terms of "therapy" or asylum. But too late for that one, huh? Went straight to that; barely any questions asked about what was "missing." Or, why one was able to sit still with plenty of concentration crafting, while also thinking in two systems of thought. But is that not weird? That sitting still and with enough concentration to craft what one saw with one's own eyes, was not even thought of as possible once before. And why not? Because thinking in systems' thinking was so convoluted, or so it seemed. Again that depended on what system of thinking one was first aligned to, systemic or structural. And then once one learned how each of these re-interpreted one's home life? Oy, vey! It could become confusing!

One was supposed to be able to hold two thoughts alongside one another were they not? Yes, they were. And some would even conceptualize this as, just what was normally expected. Nothing to it. Nothing to "what though"? Everybody was supposed to be hard-wired to hold more than one thought at one time. And we keep thinking so, even today. In the daylight hours, what seemed strange during the night, no longer was. But we needed to be aware of that. And why might that be? There were only certain times when the mind seemed to act as if all of what was out there during the night contained "strangeness." Including one's thoughts, feelings, even abreactions to what one during that time of night. Is that not unusual to espy now? When we know that what takes place in our minds at night are just dreams, or contemporaneously, thoughts we had not thought that much about during the day. Or better still, preconscious warnings. But then did these not also disturb us even further? Yes, they did. And they should. They should because what is out there in our consciousness does not seem to matter as much as what these preconscious warnings seem to be bringing. And those are? Unrepressed thoughts, feelings, even ideas. Imagine that?!

If one was preoccupied with this one term, word, or even one idea and the thoughts, feelings, and reactions associated to any of these, then, was one not also hyper-focusing on the mind? And was that not preferable than not attending to them at all? But was that not also a symptom? A symptom of what? The mind's preoccupation with itself? Or the need to keep self-aware in the picture? And why might this be better than not having any sense of one's mind? Because without these then it seemed the mind was too preoccupied with itself. But how could that be? How could the mind continue to converse with itself, and keep on doing so forever? Because it could; but then it happened upon something that made it stop. And what was that perchance? An illustration that was too phenomenal not to take notice of. And, not only drew the mind to it, but held it there in its path. Which was fantastic. And why might that be? Because it was a complete image (imago from the Latin) that held wonder, splendor, even more words than could be, all within this sight. All that within an image and within that there were all these interiorities in there too; which all seemed to need Enlightenment. But what for? Had we not studied this period of time in our lives in minute detail? And had we not also agreed that this period of our lives symbolically represented us? Even captured a part of our selves? And that was why it seemed too illustrious too? Possibly. Now, why might that be?

During that time when Enlightenment prevailed we were learning quite a bit about ourselves. Were we not? But that depended on what motivated us to even look at this period of time. Was it the illustrations themselves which attracted the mind to this period of time? Or was it perhaps that a mind needed to be acquainted to it? And that was enough for it, a superficial acquaintanceship. However, for those of us who actually wanted to learn a bit more about this visual space, i.e., perception, then being able to see a cover and know what was stored within it? Or even behind it? That took more than just a cursory look at it; it took knowledge and scholarship, and knowing this visual field inside and out, did it not? Yes, it did.

We had: not only given this area of our lives an in-depth look, and really given it a great deal of thought; but also had we not, we would have remained in the Dark Ages or in Pagan time. And yet, here we are in the 21st century trying to reconnect to these. And desperately trying not to upset anyone who happened to remain in either of these; but that was also when another realization was made. Choices counted, and really good ones came from learning. Did they not? Yes, they did. But so did learning in and of itself. This, though, invited having to look at more than one side; in fact, this instigated education in the formal sense that we know of it today. Rather than how it was once conceived of, as just what happens normally as one lived out one's life, and there really was not any accounting for what one had done during their lifetime; just that they had lived longer than others. But that should have been enough. Because as each generation lived, existing on the land as they had this also entailed they had learned something. Survival, or how to procreate, something which showed they had existed; and they had been able to live or tolerate "life" long enough to pass on something to the next generation. Now had they not been able to do that? Well, we really do not know what would have resulted, now, do we? No, but we do have the capability to infer, do we not? Yes, we do. But how could that be? How could we go from not knowing to certain knowing, and then back to inferring that we could actually fill-in those gaps? Without also remembering why? We needed to learn. And learn we must, or else "die"? All right so one did learn. One learned what had been self-taught. But what about that which either came normally or undisturbed? Was this also valued? Yes, it was. It was conceptualized as incidental; in the positive sense of this term. Yet, this was the eye-opener for us, was it not? Yes, it was. If we kept the imago in our foreground, just like we were supposed to, then it meant we had to look through it; those of us here on the sensate-side of life.

Innately, when this is triggered it acts as a mechanistic response should: it takes the lead. But, it also prevents us from adapting too. And as a very sophisticated warning system; it essentially, alerts us to our "red-flags." And though these may change with time, or due to other circumstances, they still remain one of our best defenses. They stay raised, i.e., on high alert till the danger passes; and to dispose of this system too readily or too quickly would, not only cause more harm than good, but it would be to our detriment as a species to do so. But why might that be? Partly, it is due to our dependency on them. We have learned that when they are raised, triggered, we already seem to know why. And because we do, then when they are raised we assume they are a normal reaction to repetition, i.e., having to be aware of them over and over again. This type of warning-forewarning system also troubles us. Because it continues to rise "in the past in the new moment," as though a part of us never forgets, nor should it. But when it does this (as a part of human nature and their repertoire of responding), it makes it seem as though that is all to this reflex.

A reflex is supposed to remind us and be relied upon in case of danger. But it becomes troublesome when this is the only reaction one depends on even when there is no longer any peril to speak of. Then not only does this type of innate responding continue to be empowered by this circular motion, it continues to respond because of the way it is hard-wired, i.e., housed in a closed system. And it is in this closed-system for a reason; it is there to protect us. And though this mechanism is hard-wired to respond when we are in peril, once the threat is removed it is also supposed to stop signaling we are in trouble or in danger. But, suppose this reflex does not know how to do this? Suppose as a defense mechanism it does not know that the danger has been removed, or that our life is no longer in peril, then what? Then it is up to us to know that what is out there either is no longer a threat, or what had been a threat is no longer a danger. And then taking this new knowledge, and making better informed choices; even if they are informally-based.

So now that we know how our vestibular system can be concussed, and what it is like when it is, we may also know how long it takes for this system to re-stabilize. But while we are waiting for it to stop resonating, it continues to emit waves. Waves which still cause us to feel as if we are caught in it; seasick, even though we sighted this image, it was taking place out in outer space; which was quite odd. When supposedly seasickness was not the reason why one felt this reeling sensationor this back and forth movement. But it happened that this was exactly what was being transmitted through the airwaves, as aftershocks to those transmissions.

One could feel these back and forth movements (as vertigo) rather than rocking to and fro, then it also means it either is in remission, or it is actually at the very end its transmission. Either way, these wavelengths actually serve to remind us what it may have been like to be locked away, and "celled."

Cells, remember are defined in-utero. When they are in the beginning stages of new life. That is when they begin to divide into specialities, even sub-specialities which continue to divide genetically, until they are barely visible to the naked eye. And then they each take on a life (or will) of their own. And this includes not only this vestibular system, but each of the separate organs that are ill-effected when they are resonated upon due to this type of concussion. But what exactly were we concussed by again? Oh, right that image. The one that continues to haunt us. But why should it? It was only a nocturnal sight, and it was not there for very long in its original state. Now was it? So, again, what was keeping us from re-settling internally? That's right. That big booming blast of sound which came from out of nowhere. And then simply disappeared without a trace. But it did leave a trail, did it not? But that trail was not as easy to dispose of as that first cloud was. So what did that mean? Nothing really; only that, since that cloud was decombusted so easily, it also seemed as if there was nothing remaining to talk about or discuss. Ah, but that is what clinched it, was it not? That thought that there was nothing there for further discussion. Because, as I just mentioned, any thought given to any kind of substance even if it is just "air time" means one haa given it some amount of attention. And any attention, even to the simplest of elements, such as air or water, or temperature, or height, literally elevates them to a sensation. And sensing these is the most rudimentary function of our bodies, basically due to their hard-wiring. Although this is the primary means by which most of us operate, i.e., through our physical body and through sensation, it leaves out one very primary (if not crucial) way of interacting with one's world or even that of another's, perception.

Perception actually over-ruled sensation for quite some time. And until that could be sorted out, then, war and uncertainty abounded (internally, of course); but, while this type of internal process was taking place, another force which was much stronger than any other stepped in. And that was belief, a firmly held system. But this tiny little world held more in it than anyone could have imagined; which was why it was so powerful, and also why it was at times difficult to discern. So what did this tiny speck of a world hold within it? It held within it certainty that it did not even have to be acknowledged. It was just there, and that was all that mattered. But it also held foreknowledge that whatever took place was destiny, which then became prophetic. And therefore, it no longer was super-ordained. It was meant to be just an ordinary way in which one observed the world, and kept on watching what took place "out there" as if it belonged to somebody else. Thereby, not only was one keeping one's distance and their objectivity, i.e., their cool-headed levelness, but their subjectivity as well. Nothing wrong there; except that, if one chose to remain in this worldview, distant, cool, and level-headed, then one was mistaken time and time again. Now why might that be true now, when we have all this certainty?

To be held within this was like being in a whirlwind caught unawares. And yet It was supposed to be an additional lesson on life. There were elements out there in the environment which were also affecting it, i.e., this mindset. Which is why they seemed so "wishy-washy" and pleasing all in one package; but, to stay in this position and also remote too, not only seemed foolish, but literally formed a chasm which was more than destructive. But not to everyone, right? There were only some interested in this internal view, while others were "different." Different, though, is also what separated us in the early beginnings of life.

Being thought of as being different or unique was a mainstay in this type of internal belief system. It was also one way for it to remain true to itself. But if it continued to remain in this stationary front, and only hyper-focused on what it was doing (or not), then it was showing a weakness. That it could survive the elements unaffected; and that it could do so with encouragement. So what did that mean for us here on Earth?

On Earth, remember, we hear sound faster than we see the image or the sight which evoked that motion in the first place. So while we are waiting for the sight to catch-up with our ears, we are left looking for exterior clues. That is, what made that sound appear quicker than the sight? Or, perhaps, why did that sound percuss after that image appeared to be destroyed rather than in front of it? Forewarning us of the destruction, rather than us having to wait passively by while watching that entire scene be displaced. But that was just it, was it not? The wind that confronted that airy cloud seemed passive at first; it was just shifting this wispy cloud from the front to the middle, leaving that larger one just where it sat, intact. And while this bit of wind blew that smaller, wispier cloud and its material apart, the eyes watched it all; as if mesmerized by it all. That is, until a new movement disrupted that. And that was another adverse reaction to the winds causing that kind of commotion. But it was also a part of the conditions. It seemed balmy out there, and also peaceful; when then set the mind at ease till that wind came in from out of the north, and dispensed with that scene completely.

Then it was colder. But it was also darker. These seemed to emit no immediate danger, or movement was taking place out there. And yet we knew this to be an inaccurate account, did we not? And why was that? Because even though there were no clues for the eyes to pick up on, our ears had been rung from that blast of sound air; which then led to our ears perking up. Although they were already fine-tuned to the night and its airwaves, they still felt shocked by that very night. As was mentioned earlier, they had been tuning in to the silence that was out there. And while they had been, they too were hypnotized by all the calm that was apparently there. Because, even though that wispy cloud was displaced as it was, it was done without any noise or sounds that a human ear could trace. But that did not mean they could not hear; in fact, this was the biggest "night error" of them all.

The ears heard more than they let on, and this included both daytime and nighttime earth-tones and sounds. This of course meant that once they had recognized that sonic boom as something unearthly, even at that time of night (or early morning) there was nothing which could force them to change, i.e., "unlearn" this. It was heard clearly and one knew that it was a perfectly manmade sound; because it was diabolical. It literally broke through the silence, but it also broke the sound barrier, just by association. It was the same as a jet propelling itself at an airspeed which was abnormally faster than one would expect. Which of course, if one heard this and knew what it signaled, shaking and vibrations from this type of air displacement, then not only would it force the air to feel woozy, but it would jar that inner ear vestibular system; thus, sending a signal to an even larger organ, the stomach. And then when this was alerted, i.e., the nerves within it were electrified, it too could feel this airwave and the light waves as one big vibration. Which then in turn, made it feel as if it was spinning; which added to the turbulence; but then once that feeling was felt, then the three of them could begin calming each other once again. And thus, return to homeostasis: a steady-state of being after having been ruptured just by this super, sonic airwave disturbance and by being able to see this night vision as clearly as one did.

So these three inner organs, the eyes, the vestibular system, and the stomach begin to calm. And as they do, they also sense the scene differently. That is the vibrations which had made all of that commotion originally, made that image appear as if it was at a standstill. Then when the wind pushed those forward moving clouds into a different position, only one remained in the front; the other, moved backwards toward the center. Thus, in their departing, not only did they literally make space in between them, but by doing so, they literally differentiated themselves from each other. One was lighter, the other heavier. One was airy, while the other seemed solid, i.e., condensed and darker. Their being able to be moved and unmoved also lent to their image as cloud-types; which also meant they were partnered with Earth and her atmospheres, not the Moon's as was earlier reckoned. But though they were aligned with Earth and her science that did not mean we were not unaffected by the Moon or her glow. Because with her assistance, not only was that original image captured as one whole slow, moving picture, which just happened to appear in the northern hemisphere that night; but due to her complexion that night, they seemed inter-connected. That is her radiation poured forth onto them, and this then showed in their interiors. In the case of that darker cloud, this radiance was apparently absorbed on the posterior side of it, which helped it to be illuminated as darker than its brother, the lighter, wispier one. But this too was an error, and apparently a rather large one.

The Moon was not radiating its own light; it was reflecting the solar rays that were out there in deep space. But for those two clouds to be seen as they were across that Moon's face, meant they were being radiated twice. Once due to their posterior position, from the backside of the Moon's reflection, and anteriorly, by the solar rays as they were reflected back to them after they had entered the Earth's surface. But this rebounding-rebinding motion seemed irrelevant at first. Because they were just two simple clouds, floating nearer to Earth, and therefore they were essentially not in danger of being destroyed just by the Moon or "her glow," but they could be if the Earth's surface grew warmer, or colder; and that is what alarmed us the most. That our ozone layer was no longer as capable of protecting us as it once was. However, our ability to see those clouds receiving twice the dose of radiation than what is typically seen that late at night should have also alerted us to the smog that has been lurking out there for quite some time. But the glow coming off that Moon should have also informed us of this as well. Because of their color, it was not clean. Through osmosis they had actually semi-filtered that particular airstream – but it still showed a mixture of yellow-brown and white. Which is also what contributed to the quality of the air, and also how those light waves were able to be emitted out in space that night; semi-transparent air particles which not only contained moonshine, but also all the other particulates which were also floating out there too. So that when these reached the eyes as light waves, they were seen as both lovely and also having nothing to them. They were just light waves which had caused the eye to pay attention to them, and not to be too disturbed by their exterior appearance. They were just there as just another lovely night vision. And their interiors, the particles that made them able to be perceived by the eyes were minimized. But it also made them semi-visible, which was both good and bad news to us here at ground level. When they finally entered (re-entered) the Earth's atmosphere, these air waves not only gravitated the eyes toward the spot where that image was seen (i.e., under one's ozone layer), but because of the condensed quality that was in them, we could literally see them. Not just as air that moved around the Earth normally, but as smog that had infiltrated our air zone. But who talks about this type of air pollutant as if it is lovely to look at? Nobody, because to do so would be ludicrous. Have we not been working toward destroying this evil in our environment so that all of us can breathe easier? Yes, but; perhaps, even cleaner too? But then the downside of that would be if we removed this, then we would never see clean air. It would be invisible to us. Then we would not see how the clouds and the Moon had made that lovely impression on our sight.

In come these light waves which are semi-transparent. And they bring with them light which has been radiated by the Sun, and reflected by the Moon which are then received here on Earth. And they are considered transparent, because they have no substance in them to speak of; they are just light waves. But also due to the distance in which all of this takes place, by the time they reach Earth and her atmosphere, these light impulses are extinguished. They have emitted their light. Their chemical emissions have reacted, and sent this type of solar energy across many miles of airspace so that by the time they reach Earth again, they have decomposed, recomposed, and composed themselves several times over to finally come to rest on the surface of the human eye; but they also infiltrated the Earth's surface too, warming it. And over many centuries of this, not only were these light transmissions radiating heat and light onto the Earth's surface; but as it rotated, these solar rays continued to emit solar energy which was captured by the land, the waters, and anything else they happened to come in contact with.

The capability of the Sun to transmit relentlessly, should have alarmed us many moons ago (no pun intended). But it had not. Instead, what it did as most of the planets, stars, and satellites and other objects out in deep space did, was continue doing what they were apparently constructed to do: emit whatever peculiar particles and chemical compounds they were made of out into the atmosphere. And then eventually, if they happened to enter the Earth's atmosphere, they either would continue to decompose or turn into dust, depending on their acceleration. So then, if that was the case, then how did those few solar rays enter the Earth's orbit, and not become "nothing"? In other words, how did light beams continue to penetrate the Earth's ozone layer and reach the Earth's surface, even though there was this upper-layer

shield? Which was supposed to protect us and keep us safe?
But that was just it. If too much sunshine reached us at all
hours, day and night, then we would not be constructed as
we are today. That is as a human species, we would all look
very different than we are now. But since we are not, then it
must be this planet's fault.

The Earth

Our having to live under her roof for such a long time,
must have affected us. And we know that it has, because not
all of us live on the five continents as one. In fact, our ability
to migrate from different regions on this planet Earth has not
only globalized us; but also re-settled us, day after day, year
after year till finally we no longer needed to explore her
surface. We had hunted and gathered enough of her external
resources to know why this planet was meant for us. But
also why there were limited resources out there for us to
gather and to utilize over and over again. However, one of
the drawbacks for this multi-use planet is that eventually we
would use it up. So then that meant we needed to draw our
attentions back to ourselves, and determine what we could
do with what we had, so that future generations would have
something left of this planet for their use. And that meant
one went inside, internally and asked those really difficult
questions, such as: What is our purpose in life? And why are
we here? Why are we not on Mars or Jupiter? Or some other

planet in our solar system? What is it about Earth and what she provides to us that maintains us here on Earth? And why is it still so important for us to keep her viable? This last one seemed easy enough to answer: If she dies, so do we. But is that not an oversimplification? Yes it is. But, just because it appears to be that way, it does not make it so. That is, it does not make it real.

We have a symbiotic relationship with our planet Earth. She provides the cover, i.e., the dome under which all of us live under. And without this, we speculate that we would not only look different than we are today, as living breathing animals, but we may not even be here at all in our human forms. Instead, what we could still be the amphibious-like creatures that we once were. Or, even smaller still: just single- cell amoebae swimming about in one big aquatic pond, until the temperatures changed dramatically. And then, we transformed into "monsters." But without her resourcefulness, we might still be in these earlier formations. Now would that not be strange? But that still does not discuss in full our part in this symbiotic relationship, now does it? No it does not. But why is that? What is it about disclosing how we take of her needs that mandate "bulk" rather than brawn? Basically it has to do with our value system, but it also has to do with our understanding of her.

Earth is our planet, and without knowing how she operates to sustain us, we would not know what she needed in return from us to replenish her. In other words, did she need more earthlings who understood the planet as a whole? Or did she need sub-specialists? People who had the wherewithal to study her, so they knew how to sustain her; but also knew there was a major difference between sustaining her and sustaining them. But knowing this was what caused the biggest spiritual rift of them all. And even though by 21st century standards we know this, even acknowledge that it bears a great deal on how much "green" we see out there; it never seems to reach enough ears (unlike that sonic boom noise that was heard loud and clear that night). That sound not only resounded that night, but it literally disturbed, and re-distributed those sound waves, causing that air to break into tinnier airwaves, until eventually they no longer were heard by the human ear. And these in turn, became nothing; just like that wispier cloud which was destroyed previously. But that air was not "nothing" was it? It was positively charged with dust or some other finite particles which had gathered that night in that airstream. That was how we were able to see it at first, i.e., the air, and then when it disappeared, we "worried" about it; or at least tried to grapple with why that thinner, wispier cloud was made so elusive: it was there and then it was not. And though we could fight (figuratively speaking) to try and regain an image of it again, it was long gone; and we rationalized that it was due to *that* wind, the one which came in from the west. This then caused that turbulence, i.e., the "whirlwind effect," which we caught with our very own eyes. And though this simple air maneuver was caught by our ocular system, it still did not register that it was gone. Not until that air space was cleared of that disturbance, then one could literally see the space where that flurry had taken place. It was only then, and only then one could see that darker image, i.e., the heavier cloud that hung in that lower right quadrant of airspace. So once that was firmly imprinted in the mind, then two more re-semblances took over.

One was the original Moon with that milky-brown appearance, still moving across the horizontal line. And as it continued to travel, its discoloration continued also. So that meant the upper atmosphere must have been discolored; which had nothing to do with the clouds and their coverage that night. It was just the Moon reflecting the Sun's solar rays at that time of night as it slowly drifted across the night sky. But without those two clouds it did not seem to be as appealing. And therefore, dissolved (i.e., was dis-membered). So, in other words, it did not take as completely as it would have had it had these two additional features. Which then meant for it to be recalled in its entirety, one had to imagine what those two clouds must have contributed to that moonscape, i.e., to make that picture as a whole reappear all at once. But that seemed impossible. Not only because that wispier cloud was long gone, but even in an attempt to remember it, there was no use. Which then meant it had not left a deep enough impression in the mind's eye long enough for it to resemble itself there as a whole; before it could be retrieved. So what was one to do, *if* one wanted or desired to reconstruct that particular picture? Start from where it impacted the eyes the most (i.e., in the occipital lobe region) and the memories of it there. And then recollect it from there.

The Moon was milky-brown, and was caught by the eyes moving slowly across the northern night sky. Then, besides its color and its movement there was the thin wisp of a cloud which also distracted the eye simply by its reverse movement; which was in stark contrast to that original wind's motion, which then caused the eye to catch that wind-sweeping motion. And verify that the air was moving that cloud in an opposing direction. And it had done so alone, which meant that it was the stronger of the two invisible forces (i.e., the two winds). This then in turn equated to "brute strength." But why would one need to be impressed by this factor, when all we are speaking to is reconstructing this one sight? Because without being able to literally see how these two airstreams mixed that night, we would not have seen how those two clouds separated, and how this also led to the thinner cloud being swirled in such a way that we could see the turbulence. This also allowed us to see how their combining movements made that cloud appear separate from that larger, darker cloud; before it was completely removed from our sight. And though all of this took place in a matter of seconds, it was caught by the eyes before that scene went away. So did those details help? Or only confuse the re-assembling of it? Obviously, it confused the remaking of it. Because of its turbulent motion; when that lighter cloud disappeared, there was no point to repeating it, because it held the lightest aspects of that scene. But through its undoing, there was more clear air to be seen before the next "eye action."

In this one, there not only is opened space for more of the Moon's glow to appear, but once that air space re-appeared, not only could one see how white those clouds were in stark contrast to the Moon and her glow; but also how seeing this space uncluttered also contributed to the slow moving action which also affected that first out-take. She continued to move purposefully. Mainly because she was just following her path, i.e., her orbit around us. This remembrance then re-constituted some of that earlier illustration. But it also brought forth the clouds' cover, which supposedly held the air particulates which were discoloring that Moon's face. When in fact, it was the atmosphere; and even though this fact is very obvious in the daytime, it is not as easy to recognize when one is ecstatic or even excited by this image as it slowly moved through that night's sky. Now how do these two human processes feed into "remembering"? For one, this startle response is normal. And secondly, seeing something as unusual or as beautiful as this Moon and her accompaniment, is what arouses our eyes to pay attention to her. These then combine to inform the sensate mind, and the mechanistic aspect of it to record what it sees there. And because we have this unique ability to automatically take pictures, but not necessarily the ability to differentiate them into sub-categories, i.e., what is exotic or different from that which is unusual or normal, we have a storage space: a Memoria in which they are housed collectively. And then in order for these later to become a panoramic view of a love scene, we need these to be sequenced, and re-sequenced in some orderly fashion, so they make sense to a majority of us.

Love scenes of this kind, though, are typically benign and tend to disappear almost as quickly as they are made. However, even though they tend not to last beyond their initial appearance, they still continue to reverberate, which is good for us to note. And why is that? As was earlier discussed, light vibrations which occur out in space can travel for miles till they eventually meet another obstacle. And in the case of this love scene, it was a set of human eyes which happened to be watching the Moon attired as she was, traverse the night sky in silence. And the way in which she was clothed, not only drew or allured the eyes to watch her, but even her sultry color kept the eyes attuned to her. So was this just an affectation, the kind that draws one near to it but does not last for very long? Possibly. Anything is possible when one puts one's mind to it, right? But that does not fully explain the need to keep the Moon in the foreground, while also trying to re-construct that image pre-wind gust.

Turmoil

It is quite difficult to stop the winds' movement. In fact, it does not even seem reasonable to expect that they would. They were, after all, a part of living here on Earth. Which is why their appearance is not that strange or odd; and for the most part, we take them for granted. And since they are just a part of the Earth's atmosphere, they just whip through her and touch whatever they happen to come in contact with, willy-nilly. But when one is trying to see them at night, or in a different way than the typical, it almost becomes futile. So why waste the time trying to remember how they moved together that night decombusting that thin, wispy cloud? What was the point for that? The point, was so that once one saw how the air moved in those two opposing directions, one could also *see the air move*, unobstructed by anything out in space while in the background, the Moon lit this activity all alone. And then while this was taking place, one just sat and they watched. Then while all of this was taking place, one was also supposed to be tending to this other view: the one which was left after those winds blew that whole scene apart.

That other scene was the upper half of that Moon, which appeared fuller once the top-section of it was literally cleared of that sliver of cloud. This then made it possible to discern what was in the lower half of it: The larger, darker cloud which remained in the lower, right-hand quadrant of that Moon's face. And this unobstructed view, then led one to see this cloud's form as a cumulus cloud. And its position (which was as the lead object) never even appeared to have been affected by that eastward moving wind. However, it had. Because it had been stalled by that counter-motion, and when the eyes detected this, they too caught this as "non-movement." And this made it look like it laid in wait for the next movement; but it did not have to wait for very long. Within a matter of minutes, a Nor'easter blew in with its power and its might, and blew that cloud back toward the center. Basically making it look as though one was closing a "black curtain" across that Moon's face; and where total darkness was experienced for the very first time that night.

Once that smaller, lighter cloud was discarded, and there was this empty space just above that larger cloud (and one could see this plainly), it was also quite obvious that no matter how hard one tried to reconstruct it, it was no use. That flimsy wisp of a cloud did not have enough active particles within it to be remembered in whole. So that it could be remembered in the occipital lobe. And then retrieved from there once more so that it could be retold, storied by words alone; but, if one desired or wanted to recreate it and the part that it played in the winds' deconstruction of it, one needed to be graphically gifted. In other words, able to transcribe it in plenty of time so that when it came time to put it into words, one could. Or if one could not, then just leave it as a lesson learned, i.e., once one saw how those two winds demolished that thin, upper atmospheric cloud, leave it as that. And just remember that winds which confront one another, may combust whatever happens to come in-between them; and that there is no stopping the winds. So when that larger Nor'easter came in and blew that larger cloud into the darkness that already lay out there, we should have been forewarned. But we were not. In fact, due to its strength and its capability it literally took that larger cloud as it was constructed, and moved it into the darkness; which also made it seem darker than it actually was out there. And why was that? Once that smaller cloud was no longer there, and there was this emptied space, then when this wind blew in from the northwest, there appeared to be nothing to stopping it. And since this seemed similar to what had just happened between those two winds, it also looked as though that larger cloud should have been demolished; but it was not. All that appeared to happen to that cumulus cloud was it was displaced. Literally, it was pushed as a whole entity and moved back to where it had originally came, and that was in the east.

So in comes this Nor'easter. And when it moved that large cumulus cloud toward the center of that scene, it literally eclipsed the Moon. It seemed radical that a wind of this might could move a solidly constructed object such as this cloud across the front of this Moon, and shut out its moonlight. And it was radical to think this, until it was realized that this wind had nothing in front of it, and it could basically move that cloud unobstructed. However, the result of that movement, the darkness that enveloped that Moon was a culmination of movement, i.e., one front moving toward the other. There was darkness on the posterior side of that nocturnal image which also was trailing this nighttime sight. And it too was converging into this relatively small space of time. So when that wind moved that cloud from its anterior position, i.e., from that forward position back to where it had come, they met the darkness which appeared to lay in wait as well. Then, this closing made it look as though there were no competing forces coming to meet in this one space, because it simply happened. And why was that? Why was a force of nature, such as this Nor'easter and its ability to move that substantially large cloud to the other side, without causing any disarray seen as an equal to that trailing darkness? Because when they met midway, all they did was close that curtain of dark matter together. And by the time the eyes registered this, they had normalized it as what typically happens when two airstreams of this type meet.

Nothing much to write home about, right? Yet the way in which these two "opposites" re-connected with each other in slow motion, not only showed the speed in which a heavily-laden object (such as this wind with this cloud) could move; but that seeing it bring that cloud with it to a place where it could meet this other airstream (which was also laden with heavier air) was quite a sight. When they met, they literally meshed, i.e., over-lapped. This then provided a screen. A screen of such magnitude that it literally obliterated the Moon from our sight, and it remained firmly in this place, as a gathering of this kind. So as that screen system settled itself in, it was also demonstrating a unique human principle: differentiation. It was showing us that it was not the same airspace as the one that was there before. And it did this by closing off the Moon directly from our sight. And because it did, it also blocked out what light remained there, leaving the air there without any light waves of any kind except dark ones; which we could further discriminate as, negative energy. The air still pulsed, i.e., it was still lively, but what our eyes saw was complete unadulterated darkness; which made no sense at all, until one looked and saw how that cloud coverage was completed without decombusting those clouds. Then not only was this more intriguing to the eyes as they watched how that was accomplished, very slowly; but having seen this and how that was accomplished by two divergent airstreams out it nature, then one could determine that was all there was to making that screen appear there as it did. However, the assumption was that eventually that black screen would dissolve, but it did not. In fact, the longer that it remained there in that space, the longer it gave the Moon time to escape. But since when did the Moon need "time" or need to escape, when all that it was doing was traveling through our night sky unencumbered?

We know that these airstreams do not even come close to touching the Moon's space. So how could we imagine that they did? Or that what they were carrying, their "baggage" if you will, blocked those light airwaves from ever reaching Earth? Because they did; they blocked the light rays, due to what was in them. But within them was also condensed. Filled with more than just air, they held molecules, which were composed of chemicals. And these chemicals, additives, caused that air space to be contaminated; not by "bad" air per se, but by air that could literally remain stagnant and unclear. And so because they could act as a filter and screen out the Moon's light, then it seemed they were only there for one reason, to keep her from being seen "unattired." But that too was what was so alluring.

Here were these two upper air currents which had brought this screen into place. They then leave this object between us and the Moon. Nothing wrong with that, *except* that also seemed to limit us. It kept us from seeing what else was taking place behind that screen. And it acted as a prohibitor. Which, if we were no longer curious, might suffice as an end result; but that obstacle and where it was placed in particular, directly in front of that Moon's face, not only drew more energy to it rather than away from it; but it also seemed to mesmerize. Strange how that blockade would draw one's eyes to it, rather than away. But this is why. When that image of that Moon first appeared there, as it was dressed, it was lovely to look at. In fact, it was quite striking; that is why it imprinted on the eyes the way that it did. And though that thin wispy cloud was dissolved, and the air became all-a-flutter, i.e., in turbulence, it still maintained its eye appeal. In other words, it was still beautiful to the eyes to behold. And when that airstream re-settled, and that heavier cloud was still there (in that lead position and in that lower, right-hand quadrant), the Moon still held the eyes captive. So not only did the eyes recapture her there, but they also saw that she had not moved during that combustion. But it was darker out there than it was before, which could only mean the air had changed just by that shift. Because what that meant was whatever was in that lighter cloud had now caused that upper air current to cloud. And due to this collision either these air particulates fell or went skyward; or they continued to twist about separated by this motion. But during this commotion, this air was dusty.

This decombustion was quick and relatively over, before that Nor'easter blew in and shifted that scene. But in that brief split-second of time (before it arrived), there was a glimpse of the Moon as that airstream was resettling. Which is when it was noted that it was there; but it was there with only the cumulous cloud still attached to it. This was odd, because the assumption was that those two airstreams would have made that larger mass disappear, but they had not; which then meant that cloud was built to withstand this kind of air pressure. Which was possible; but by seeing that cloud lay untouched as it was, it should have also alerted the eyes to perk up. And they did. Because when they did, and they saw how clearly that Moon looked with only that milky-brown film *still* in front of it; then it meant there was something terribly wrong within the Earth's upper atmosphere. Not that what happened here on terra firma had anything to do with that! But it did. Seeing that film across the Moon's face only enticed the eyes. But it should have alerted us here on Earth that our airspace was contaminated AND that there were no definitive lines between here and her. Which then should have also forced us to look at what we were doing (or not) to clean up those transmissions, the ones that happened to filter down into our shared airspace.

Why had those two airstreams not caused that airspace to be clear? Such as what one would expect when the air's been cleared by something that has the ability to move such as these two did. But that was just it, was it not? That airspace was never going to be clear completely because of the chemical compounds that naturally occurred out there in the air The Sun's chemical reactions traveled through that space to reach us, and when they entered this part of our upper atmosphere, they had already traveled through the ozone layer to reach us. And our interception of them here on Earth not only informed our eyes, i.e., see these as light waves but as bandwidths as well. But these bands of light were not always apparent, because of the way they were clumped into two colors, white or yellow. And since they were, then seeing that milky-brown film across the Moon's face, almost matched one color scheme, i.e., the one toward the white. However, this near match (though beautiful to watch) did not even come close to the message that it was sending. Seeing that type of milky-brown appearance meant those airwaves were still disturbed by the sum total of the Sun's solar rays penetrating the Earth's shield, i.e., the ozone. Which either meant the Sun was closer to the Earth's surface (which it was at that time of year), but that its heat too was contributing to that late night appearance; that is, the temperature of that particular airstream was warmer that night than usual. But these types of molecular particles literally ate away at this upper crust without us really knowing that they were; which contributed to this upper layer eroding as it was. And while we here on Earth still needed the Sun and its solar energy to reheat us, and to light our surface twenty-four hours a day, we also needed to pay attention to what was happening out in outer space too with the way in which our heat was being re-dispensed. So then that meant even though those few solar emissions entered our atmosphere, and worked their magic on us, we also needed to realize how they functioned to inform us.

We cannot stop the Sun from shining, nor should we because it not only provides heat, but also light. In fact, with its ability to dispense itself night and day, we have learned how powerful solar energy really is. And that without it, as some have noted in the distant past, the Earth would be in complete darkness (or at least that was a presumption that was held at one time). Now I am not so sure, especially if this solar system was constructed in one big bang. And the result of that was matter of two kind, light and dark. And each time these were re-worked, either they became lighter or darker, or nothing at all. However, even though that makes sense as far as "light waves" are concerned; that still does not fully explain how the air knows whether it is carrying light particles, condensed ones or nothing at all. But it is not up to the "air" to know this, now is it? It is up to humans and their eyes which can detect the air, and what floats through the airwaves. Is it not? And if they do not see anything out of the ordinary, then typically it means the air is undamaged. It is even possible to hypothesize that this air cleans itself just by the very fact there are these random holes in it. And that as it does, we on Earth do not need to be concerned at all about this kind of natural phenomenon.

In fact, Planet Earth by its very existence can take care of itself, except since humans appeared here on Earth, we have "amped up" the co-destruction of her. And we have done very little to slow it down, except note that it is occurring.

Mutual reciprocity

A recognition of this kind should have also made us all aware of our part in slowing her down, so that we could see and grasp that she was de-constructing herself. And to also evaluate our part in it. But this was what was so difficult to grapple with at first. How could our planet, living being that she is, continue to produce shifts and emissions which not only changed her exteriorly but interiorly as well? And that as a living planet, her internal movements not only produced surface change, but weather and also other anomalies, which could also change due to her shifts and emissions. And also as she changed, she re-combined her elements differently, and there was very little that we could do about that. In fact, it was quite natural for the Earth to shift and shape herself into whatever she had in mind. And this included, though I would guess the environmentalists would disagree with me here, how the climate and the ground on which we lived were impacted over time by her movements alone. But then, as sensate beings we have not been tracking (or living on) this Planet Earth for very long, now have we? And yet, it might feel (for some) that we are the only ones that have brought our Earth to where she is now and, not that she has brought *us* to where we are now in the 21st century.

Do we mind that Planet Earth has a life of her own? And that what she does with it also provides us with what human beings need to survive on her. And if we see that, then what she provides to us is beautiful and ready-made, and therefore should be kept this way for future generations. But this also means being able to see ALL that she has provided is a part of her doing, and that there is no other (not even us humans) to point the finger at, which is reasonable. But let us suppose we just see Earth as a place to reside, so that we can learn how to survive her? What then? Would that mean we were less cognizant of our part in her deconstruction? Or better at discrimination? That is we as human beings would know more than Mother Earth about what was causing her disruptions and her emissions which affected us. And therefore, would be the more responsible of the two with regard to how she re-consumed herself. But is that not how we all see Mother Earth today? That she is a home to us, and where we are held more accountable for her undoing. Quite an amazing arrangement, if we also did not know that as she consumes herself, more of us are also being consumed than once before. But is that not an amazing thought! She actually is the largest compost heap known to Man. And that should make us happy, if not ecstatic that she has this ability and that we are a part it. But many of us fail to recognize Earth in this capacity, or simply do not know what a compost pile is. And why might that be? Because, not all of us think at the organic level, or that Earth has this ability to break-down and re-soil her surfaces enriched by this seemingly innocuous capability. But at this level, we all play a part in her decomposition.

We heap a great deal of our garbage onto her, and then we watch unencumbered while she decomposes what we have put there. And while she works through these spoils, she generates heat. This heat then combines with the other elements, and continues to destroy these leftovers. As this process continues, then other silent or surface signs emerge from it. For example, one may smell an odor or may even see waves of heat coming from these heaps. And once these are detected, they can then be screened by our eyes and our noses. As either something that is either repugnant, "spoiled" (i.e., rancid), or what a compost pile should smell like as it goes through a natural decaying process. Or we may turn once again to our eyes and see how much heat is being radiated from this composting process, and obtain from them "an eye determination." Heat that is visible must have something else in it which causes it to emit waves of heat. But what exactly? What causes those heat waves to move in such a way that the eyes can detect that they are there? And that they are heat? And not just odor molecules? Could it also be possible that these self-same "heat waves" contain both heat and odor, and that is why they can be seen? Which is what makes them very different than seeing these self-same air particles as light which had been filtered through the upper atmosphere; they are even different than those two clouds and their substances. They are also different from these kinds light particles, because they transport temperature molecules which have been mixed with other products which have yet to be re-consumed by Earth. But, here is what is so inviting about watching these heated air elements: Within them they hold the leftovers of that refining process. But the soil, and all the other creatures which contributed to that decomposition? They too hold this same gaseous material in them, but not in the same manner that the air does. Because once these air-borne particulates reach the air, they either burst or become a part of another; that is, they are either inhaled by something else that is out there, or re-absorbed by an unseen force, such as a wind. And through this they become a part of Nature's plan. But also, they are disbanded from that compost pile, never to return to it.

This seems pretty simplified that all one had to do was heap a pile of matter together and then watch unencumbered while it composted itself into solids, gas, and waste. While only noting the heat element and how it seemed to be disbanded, before looking at what it had done pre-reabsorption. But is that also not the oddity? That those heated molecules could escape virtually unnoticed? But that was just it, they were not. In fact, when these air molecules combined with these other inert materials, they began to "eat away" at what was lying there. And as they churned, they made heat (i.e., the gaseous side of these molecules). And then they virtually turned whatever they touched into a liquid mess. This particular part of the metabolic process, though, was also working to redefine what remained there in that compost pile. And so each time that there was heat, it was also allowing more gases to leave that pile; causing it to shrink. But what was carried up into the open air, each time they escaped was different too. Because their emissions were re-composting something different, depending on what still remained there in that heap, and also on the kind of material that lay there waiting to be de-composed. And as with any metabolic process, this kind of decomposition took time. But what about that odor, i.e., that smell? Why was it detected as it was? Did this too not have to do with what was there in that compost pile? Yes. And yet, for those odors to be discriminated, one needed to more than just observe a compost pile decompose. It literally meant inhaling that air, and simultaneously associating it with a former smell. And if per chance, this happened to be a smell that had no association to it, or could not be recalled, then it was classified immediately as a new odor; one that had never been detected before.

This seemed self-evident. If one had never come in contact with a compost heap, where there was a mixture of organic and inorganic substances decomposing in that mound, then the odors that were being emitted there would smell unfamiliar to that nose. And in fact, most of us try our level best to avoid having any contact with anything that appears to be unfamiliar to us, and this includes odors. Why is that? As a species, there is a prescribed way of being in this world: one either survived or they did not. And since survival entailed looking out for one's well-being, then avoiding what seemed unfamiliar was the only way to accomplish this. One basically took care *never* to come in contact with anything that was unknown. This also meant over time, certain human physiological traits, e.g., Jacobson's organ, were no longer necessary for chemical detection once we were fully developed. In other words, anatomically we no longer needed this organ to fully develop so that this sensate system worked optimally. And the reason why we no longer needed this kind of organ, was due to its sub-specialty: it was constructed to detect pheromones, which were supposed to help us sniff-out another for mating purposes, and to also help us with our social behavior.

Pheromones are chemical secretions that are emitted through fluid or liquid. And we smell these fluids through our olfactory systems. So when we detect a fragrance or an odor, it does not just affect the nose, it also affects our brain and other organs which are deeply connected to this exquisite system. Virtually sending signals to all parts of our bodies, so that they know what to do with these at a very basic, instinctual, level. And that is to respond. But our ability to detect these air-borne particulates has been compromised, through our own evolution. Not just because we do not need this specialized organ or its capabilities to detect these types of secretions as human beings for locating a mate for reproduction purposes, but because as a species we have become too sophisticated to notice them. In other words, we are not rutting or are in heat, and therefore do not need to mate haphazardly (i.e., just when biologically we are primed to). Instead, we have developed subtler methods to draw a mate to us for procreation. However, pheromones are also designed to socialize us. Which seems to take us out of the ordinary realm of smell; and in fact, it does. It moves us completely into another domain, touch.

Tactile

This is one area that mammals and other animals that still retain this olfactory capability have a better understanding of than we do. They use this tactile ability not just for reproduction, but also in terms of what sensing them as they do instructs them to do instinctually sans sex. Their unique ability to detect the air with this olfactory organ allows them to note heat, i.e., differentiate the air's temperature; and it also allows them to detect another's smell. And when they do detect these differences, then it informs them on what to do next: run, hide, fornicate, or attack. And from a cognitive economist's point of view, this ability to differentiate the air and pheromones in it with this organ's assistance is the best kept secret in the Animal Kingdom. And why is that? Basically, because the ability to differentiate the air as they do, also allows them to sensate our world differently than we do; and because they can detect what is hidden in the air without any additional knowledge than these pheromones, they smell or "taste" these chemical compounds better than we do. And they note and respond almost immediately to them. And they come by this in the most natural way possible, through the way in which their bodies are genetically endowed; which is very different from us. But we also seem to share this same genetic capability when we are in an embryonic stage of life, so why are we not as capable of detecting these as these sensate beings are? Is it due to our bodies no longer needing this "hidden" capability? Or, as human beings we no longer need to sensate the air as they do? And even though we may still have this shared genetic encoding, our bodies have adapted to the environment better than these animals. And the reason for this? Our wits. We have learned how to live without this base information. But have we?

We may not rely on the air that we all breathe as instinctively as these animals do, but this is also what separates us even more from them. They use the power of smell or "taste" to communicate with each other via the air, but they also mark their territory with their odors (pheromones) so that others know where they are, by smell and pheromone detecting. But it also individualizes them too. In that the sex of their species knows who to mate with, and they know when; and they know these instinctively. And also by mating at the peak of their being, they also make their presence known; that is, they pass on or regenerate their strengths. And depending on the species, this can vary from recoiling to attacking with all of one's strength, never fearing the conditions or the consequences of those actions. They just responded. And what triggered them to respond to those signals was no longer significant. They just knew they needed to act. There was no impulsivity or abreaction, their system's response was as normal as one could obtain based on the excitation principle.

This principle, however, looks to be too simple and too straight-forward. But that's the beauty of it. Nerves touched by these chemical compounds are what simplify life, and then the choices that are made for us are basal. The nerves that were touched alchemically now know how to respond AND they do without thinking. That too is the beauty of this principle. There is no thought to stop them; and there is also no analyzing them either. It is basically just reflex. However, as humans, we like to have more than pheromones, or our hormones dictating how we react to this kind of stimulation.

In fact, physiologically, we like to think that we can over-ride their affects, even though our bodies are built to withstand their impact interiorly. But because they gender us, i.e., mark us as either male or female, they also solidify us in these human forms. Basically, sex-typing us; but along with this, expectations of how one is supposed to act based on this basal information, at the instinctual level.

So that would also mean that the information in those chromosomes somehow influenced this olfactory system in humans. And instead of seeing this system as separate from the being in which it was physically housed, it was looked upon as only for sexual engagement. To have sex for reproductive purposes only, one must smell "musky" or potent enough to startle the receiver, i.e., the receptors in the nasal cavity which responded to those smells of enticement. However, since this system no longer requires this type of sensual scenting. They have all but disappeared from our repertoire of sensing. Not just because the need to breed or to fornicate for reproductive purposes only has been mastered, but since we no longer have this kind of acuity, our ability for detecting the presence of another is dismal compared to those in the Animal Kingdom which still have this heightened capability.

They knew instinctively when one or the other sex was in heat, and they were out looking for a suitable mating partner or partners. They also knew when their territory was being threatened better than we did. And they also knew what to do when each of these situations presented itself. Quite an advantage to have over us humans, do you not think? And all, apparently, conducted through the sense of smell. This physical discrepancy though did not matter to us until there was a danger of extinction. And then it mattered to us humans that these few species could distinguish the air better than we could by only inhaling or touching the air around them. Because then they, the animals themselves could be the detectors for us, i.e., we did not need to develop this kind receptive system if our animal friends could identify for us: who needed to be mated with, how many times it was necessary to mate before there were enough offspring so one was assured their species would survive, and lastly that one knew which animal to mate with and it was not left up to chance or some other unknown. All this chemical information in just one scent? Yes, but these animals are not only sensating the air for sexual purposes only or for territorial rights only. They also use this sensing apparatus to locate warmth, which can then be used for two other needs: food and shelter.

When these animals use "warmth" as a locator, by taking the air's temperature, then they know what is in the air. And this gives them choices. They can gauge what made that air warm, i.e., the air temperature is either rising or falling, and they need to react to it due to this only. So this would mean it is either time to seek shelter or continue on about one's business. Also through this "air test," they may sense something unusual lurking in the air which alerts them that there is another kind of molecule being radiated nearby. It is another's body heat. And either this is "normal" or it is their body cooling. And these emissions enter the receiver instructing it what to do, investigate its presence or run. Or perhaps neither of these; instead, one remains in place till a certain amount of time passes. They then "test the air" once again, and when the air has once again retained its normalcy, they then carry-on with their business. However, if this scent in the air is an animal that is rotting, or it is just a heat signal indicating a live presence in the vicinity, and that is the reason for the air to be different than normal, then that would mean the animal that sensed this would also have to remain in a fixed position until they could detect which was which. This then added to their repertoire. They needed to note there was a unique smell attributed to each of these, and it was not just warmth per se. It was the scent of death (or fear for one's life) that was also being mixed in these emissions. And the ability to distinguish both was also quite phenomenal too. How would an animal know these distinctions by smell or odor alone? Because they had at one time in their life smelt it.

They had developed or refined their instincts so they would know fear as it was eliminated alchemically. Then informed by them, they were supposed to be wary of others who were not like them. And because of this exquisite sensing ability they knew this.

Hormonally, the body reacts to uncertainty normally, as a precaution to death. In fact, it actually agitates itself when it senses danger is nearby. We could even say that we have all been conditioned to respond in this manner, i.e., agitate ourselves when we think fear is lurking in the wind. But we do not actually do this as humans, do we? Mainly, due to how our bodies are hard-wired; we have lost the ability to sense the wind and the odors which designate "uncertainty" or "fear" to us. So instead of being able to sense these by odor alone, we have replaced this with *our* body's way of knowing, i.e., we know when both of these are present, because our bodies have been engineered to decode this kind of over-stimulation simply through what our body's emote alchemically. They literally become agitated when they sense something that is uncertain or should be feared. And because they do at the cellular level, there is a bio-chemical reaction to it. These cells know something is wrong; that what is taking place within this semi-closed system has been invaded by some foreign substance, and so they are responding just as they should normally. As our first line of defense; however, when they do, they are also sending out their debris, alchemically speaking. And this adds to the stimulation that the body had already acknowledged, just by noting there was something to be uncertain about, or to fear. In other words, they were excited by a stimulus.

But was this stimulus something that needed to be feared? Or was it something that we had all learned to live with? Or because there were certain species out there that had heightened sensational abilities, which were better attuned than ours to our world, we could learn from them what those were. But if we decided to do this, then it either meant we relegated ourselves to them, or we purposely demoted them; looking at them as either above us or beneath us, respectively. And yet, if we solely depended on ourselves (i.e., the human race), we would still be missing something that was happening to our environment because we would not have the same kind of capabilities as they do; and perhaps, this is a mixed-blessing. Partially, because to be stimulated by one's environment over and over again would become redundant, or worse, we would become habituated to it. And then we would no longer need to think or respond without thought, it would only be by reflex; which is how most animals (us included) respond to external stimuli. This is great news for all of us, because that shows how well we all have habituated to Earth, and her changing environments (that is those who have survived till now).

There are also some we have discovered that no longer exist, due to the environment changing more rapidly than their bodies could adapt to it. And yet, their genes did. So how did that happen? If a whole species went extinct before they were able to pass along their capabilities, then how did modern day reptiles and other creatures who detect pheromones with their tongues or in the mouth region come to be? Or was this part of Evolution's secret? It knew when certain capabilities needed to survive, and it knew which species needed these refined capabilities. So that also meant they could survive much longer in an undomesticated world better than we could. Because they still read the signs "raw."

Living in communion with Nature

Raw sign reading, though, is what our five physical senses are for. They alert us to what is happening out and inside our bodies normally. They help us to detect both environments: the internal and the external one. And they also hinder us, i.e., distract us from these as well. For instance, if I had continued to hyper-focus on that Moonscape, and had not been interrupted by that sound, then I would have been thought of as a visually-induced learner. However, when that blast of sound entered the picture, disrupting the visual and that picture I was following so closely, it made me "lose it." That is the sound and my hearing it that way temporarily distracted me from that picture's undoing. But in that span of time, when that sound wave disrupted the air, it not only dislodged me from watching only, but it also signaled that the wind was out there; and it was differently manufactured. That kind of wind did not just appear out of nowhere for no reason, it was a Nor'easter. And what it brought in was cold air moving at breakneck speed. But that was not all; it brought in destruction by its very being there. Because what it left in its wake, was absolutely nothing but cleared out air, no visual to speak of. And this mattered a great because it stunned the eyes, holding or locking them in place; while the ears began their research.

I was startled by how that sound sounded, loud and unnatural for that time of night. And then how it was registered, as a sonic boom. This meant I had had some familiarity with this "noise" before, but it was unnatural for it to be there at that time of night, and apparently in opposition to that slow, moving vision. But because of its past recognition, as an innocuous sound, i.e., a consequence of air having been broken by the rapid motion of it (air molecules virtually smashing against one another) till they broke open emitting sound waves of air; this sound was seen as what happens normally when these types of air bubbles are burst by speed and heat. This then meant, while they were re-dispersing themselves after being jolted "alive" by this kind of wind; they left sound in their wake. But the tone of that final wave when it hit the surrounding structures, including where I was, made it lethal; because of its resonance. This sound reminded me that it was not just the environment clearing itself out, it was co-manufactured by what else was out there stopping it: trees, houses, even the air itself. And from there, it became potent. Just by being able to hear that sonic boom at that time of night; because after the right side of my head registered it, it became firmly entrenched as a sound to be reckoned with. Not only because of how that sound broke the silence that was out there, but when that sound entered my awareness rather abruptly, it resounded there and also in my consciousness.

I heard this very loud, sonic boom, but it also rocked my skull. And due to the very nature of its construction, it not only was concussed by this sound on the right side of it, but it also absorbed this sonic wave from this direction too. This sound had impacted the skull, and then it was conducted internally to the organs within it: the brain and the vestibular system, but also the ancillary nerves that were also connected to this part of the body; so that they too shared in this powerful impact, and kept registering and re-registering this tone, virtually resending signals to and from inside the body, until the reverberations stopped. But this all took time. So while the head, the stomach, and the vestibular system were reeling, so were other body parts; ones that sensed something was wrong. And though they had no way of knowing, except that they were responding to being stimulated; they were still seen as having felt something adversely. And though it was not a direct result of the sound being heard through the ear (as it normally is the conducting device for sound detecting); the sound was felt internally, because it made certain nerve endings fire, "sick." And this was the by-product of that vestibular system's disruption.

Simply because of its strength, it caused that part of the inner ear system to vibrate. This then aggravated the nerves there, sending signals throughout its system. And when this system became "enraged" by that tone's wavelength and its harshness, it sent the mind-body into vertigo. The weaving in and out of focus one feels when their internal system's been disrupted, typically after a rush of information has been sent throughout this whole entire interior system. And agitated by this weaving rather than the sound that produced these motions, it (i.e., vertigo) displaces the tone. Literalizing it into a form of weakness; that is, we as humans were once thought to inhabit forests where climbing was the norm (Battles & Hudak, 2005); and even today, it is thought to be a normal part of one's human development, e.g., riding on carnival rides where vertigo is expected. And is counted on as a part of the attraction. However, even if we had some familiarity with vertigo through entertainment or our experiences of climbing, feeling it that night was not what was expected from that loud sound; unless those vibrations literally caused those symptoms for a reason. And therefore, they were warning us to stay grounded. And not to be carried away by that tone which could deafen if one was not careful. But they also served to remind us of what could happen if one only listened.

The magnitude of that loud noise was in stark contrast to what had been represented to my ears initially; which happened to be, complete and unadulterated silence. But then once this sound entered and made those waves, it was impossible to stop its "ill-effects" until the body and the mind, the whole system was able to re-settle itself. And then once it did, then I resumed trying to recapture what had happened that night to make that explosion occur as it did. Though, I knew by the time that these sensations ended, there really was no point in continuing with this type of informal investigation. That sound had been made, and although it had come in unexpectedly and had vibrated the environment, including this human body, it was gone; leaving nothing behind to attend to, but these side-effects from being impinged upon.

This was quite a significant difference from that early morning watch, where that Moonscape just happened to be slowly moving through space unencumbered by sound. But once both of these were sensated, silence and sound, and then no sound, there was a new silence to contend with. The one that remained as an after-effect outside, because it was too silent for that time of night; in other words, all the nocturnal creatures which usually make noise during the night were silenced. It was then thought that this was the "eye" of a storm. And once this passed through, then not only would there be precipitation of some kind, but a confirmation of this truth. But neither was the eye of the storm theory confirmed or the precipitation; instead all that occurred post this sound observation was the darkness which had replaced that vision. And when this was recognized, then Nature and her elements were seen as they were, in charge of our weather here on Earth: all by hearing unaided.

But was that not what being human meant? That we could detect the environment with how our bodies were hard-wired? Visually and auditorily? And that we did not need to sense it any other way than these two. But then there were our noses, and how they sensated the environment too. Yet at the dead of night when these two systems were fully aware and activated, this olfactory system was completely ignored. And why was that? Because it was not necessary to either of those two: ears could hear, eyes could see. So they were not missing anything, except how it just maintained its unique position. The nose brought in air that we needed so that we could continue to breathe. Awesome news for us humans, actually; because breathing through this apparatus countered the arousal and palpitations one was experiencing when one was excited to see that very first image traveling across that early morning night sky. And without actually being aware of this, it actually settled that vestibular system quicker than normal. But, wait?! Wasn't this sub-system only supposed to be affected when the inner ear was affected by air waves? So how did breathing in through one's nose calm it? While the body was dealing with the stimulation which had been captured by the eyes, and then by the ears and the head, it was also being infiltrated by the air. And this air was being warmed while it traveled through this semi-closed system, mixing with what was already taking place throughout the body; thus, absorbing some of the after-shock of those reverberations. It was also quite possible that this same breathing apparatus maintained a steady stream of warmed air, which virtually kept the body from over-reacting, i.e., heating beyond what it was accustomed to, while it was in this excited state. And since it could do this virtually unnoticed, silently, and typically without drawing any

131

attention to it; performing its function so there was no need to attend to it. That is, until it stopped working. But why would this sub-system be working just fine, unattended, and then make its presence known rather abruptly? Because more than likely we had "forgotten" to breathe, and without air entering our bodies through this apparatus, it alarmed us; but it was not the nose or the olfactory system per se that made that closed-off feeling to occur. Something within our own bodies alerted us to it.

The lungs had filled to their capacity with a noxious gas, and it was literally suffocating us. Granted, this may be somewhat of an exaggeration, but nevertheless whatever had caused the nose to stop its part in the ventilating of us, made it known through this sealed off and filled-up sensation. But then it was up to the body to force some other part of its ventilation system to open an airway: either by making the nose or mouth open by command, so that once again air could re-enter the body and resuscitate it. But the signal to both of these apertures had been disrupted by that particular gas filling the body, and not just the lungs.

This stimulus response not only sealed the entire airway system, but it did this normally. When there was enough air in the system, i.e., internally in the body, it stopped bringing in air from either of those two apertures, the nose or the mouth. But we did not literally feel this until we needed to breathe again, then one or the other opened as if by command. But the blocking of them voluntarily, as if one could not breathe from either the nose or the mouth was exceptional. That meant something was seriously wrong, either with the air or the transference of it from within. What within the body would signal that it needed air, but neither the nose nor the mouth responded? Was it due to the last breath that it took which held an element within it, which signaled it was "noxious air" and to open either was suicide? Or, was it the brain which deliberately silenced these two and it looked like "refusal to open up"? And because one would not, this then literally led to suffocation. And the end result, partial death. Without enough oxygen in our brain or circulating throughout those cells, it meant this part of us was dying. And we felt it as light-headedness or feeling out of focus, i.e., vertigo; and of course, this made sense because it was an abreaction from too much internal stimulation that was taking place within us. But we had also forgotten that these were typical signs of asphyxiation that the brain experienced in direct connection to not getting what it needed either; which was oxygen enriched blood. And that without this, it looked as though it was addled all because one had apparently at some point in time had forgotten to breathe, i.e., inhale through those two closed-off passageways. But if this powerful organ could not unseal those two apertures with the way that it was "feeling," then what did that mean? Neither the brain, nor any other sub-system within the body controlled what was taking place with it. There was something else: Another occupation had taken over.

The addled mind-state simply could not control the mechanistic responses of the entire body, because it too was over-loaded with responding to everything that it was feeling (electrical impulses and the chemicals coursing through it). But it too was showing that the internal circuitry was conducting itself (literally) exactly as it was pre-programmed to do. Respond to the stimuli, and then decipher or decode it the only way that it knew how to: by emitting more signals to release more chemicals; which in turn was supposed to ease the entire system, if only temporarily (which it did). However, this opiate regulatory system re-releasing each time it was supposed to, under high stress or distress, could also be disrupted. And if not accounted for, then this systemic response "backfired." Because it only served to temporarily remove the distress signal, not the actual stimulus-response mechanism; that is what made that asphyxiated state start in the first place. Was it really that one had intentionally held one's breath? Or was it the only way the body itself knew how to fend-off whatever had invaded it? Or was it perhaps the distraction of breathing that needed to be subdued? And it needed to be stopped, if only for a moment's peace (if for nothing else). But if breathing normally had become the ultimate distraction, which apparently needed to be subdued, then what did that mean? One could not breathe ever again? Or was it even more sinister or sensational than that?

That is if one could truly hold one's breath and not only feel the repercussions of this along with the other signals that were also flowing up to it, then did that not also mean one liked or preferred to feel light-headed? Otherwise, would one not stop that? Only if one could. And since that had been tried unsuccessfully, this altered state of being (while also being aware of what was surrounding one) mystified; it was even mistakenly considered "ill-equipped" to handle life as we know it today. But that was just it. Was it really that the body refused the brain or vice versa? And because of this interminable struggle, it was just better not to become involved in this, *unless* we were not just discussing bio-chemical compounds, or how one's genetics pre-disposed one to reacting to all those chemicals and connections being stimulated simultaneously. Rather what seemed to be of utmost importance was how addled one's mind could actually get, and possibly even remain that way, as though one could actually be so oblivious to needing to breathe. And therefore, making it seem that being light-headed mattered more to it, than even one's physical appearance.

And because this form of internal stimulation seemed to appeal more to the senses, then what happened to make that vision or that sound appear as they did out in the environment, neither of those two mattered. And in their stead, feeling light-headed even "spacey" became the center or focal point. If, one could essentially hyper-ventilate on purpose, as a natural consequence of being overloaded by all that stimuli and responding in kind, then was it also not possible to reinforce that? And then once one learned how to reinvent this initial light-headed state which had come out of being overloaded, then one could eventually determine if this state of being was enough to repeat (the reader is referred to Alan Watts and his studies on consciousness for further elaborations regarding this).

Although breathing became another way to alter one's state of being, and not just one's mind, there was still something about not allowing another bit of air into either of these two apertures which stymied the whole system. Why would one not open these two passageways, again? Even after feeling the ill-effects of not having done so before? Wasn't it the lack of oxygen that made one feel tense, and not just light-headed or dizzy? And would it not make more sense to just open these up so one could become clear-minded, even clear-headed again? But that was just it. It appeared that it was much easier to feel these physical symptoms (even tolerate them), than either trying to remove them or making them into more than what they were, an inability to breathe right. We could even take this one step further, and consider them as ancillary to a greater symptomology: Freud's death wish unrealized. The Psyche refused to die, even though presumably it wished to.

This internal contention only added to the tension. It did not, however, necessitate "how" one was supposed to enact this death wish. Was one supposed to actually kill their self? Or was one supposed to only think that they were dying, and as they neared or approached Death, they re-experienced Dionysian-like symptoms? And this approach-avoidance contributed to those two physical sensations: Vertigo and light-headedness. But the tension between them was also remarkable. Each time one entered this dilemma state, they either felt as if they were literally dying on the inside or they had physical problems which were not being attended to. Either way, one felt (perceived) they were not being listened to or heard internally. And so one found another solution: they chose to ignore both physical sensations completely. This then appeared to leave only one ending, to die knowing one was only somatically inclined. Hardly a way to know both sides of the human body-inner psyche division, do you not think?

So what had happened to the mind and the body to force such a split? Did one's body need to operate on its own accord? And therefore, develop its own form of control. And then once it had this "control" then it was difficult to surrender it to another, even if that happened to be to a mind, or a will? But this was the quandary. If one literally gave in or acknowledged either of these pre-existed prior to the soma, then that meant what control one had acquired would be completely lost. This then meant one had only one recourse: hold onto whatever physical prowess one had, and *never* give it up. Then ultimately it did not matter whether one had a mind or a will, the psyche component. It was unnecessary. And therefore, it never even became an issue, because the body ruled. And without it, then it seemed senseless to even engage in this type of discourse. This seemed to suffice for quite a while. In fact, it continues to this very day. Especially since now that we know how our bodies operate both at the voluntary and involuntary levels, we do not need to know if it houses a mind or a will, or that they even existed prior to this somatic system.

By referring to the soma only, were we not also "dim-witting" ourselves? That is as long as we kept the intellect at bay, then the body appeared to be safe (i.e., no more thinking was required); the body just reflected or responded to the stimuli without thought. Or, more formally speaking, once it was fated to respond as it had been prescribed or pre-programmed to respond, then all it had to do was respond. But what it was responding to, still remained a mystery without a brain. Because the brain was the executive; it controlled and apparently ruled, as well as encoded and decoded what the body was presented with. And without it, and its unique abilities, we were just empty vessels. Just bodies that collected information, absorbed it, and responded to it just like everybody else. And this kind of collective meant there would be no differences between us, or among ourselves. We would all be the same internally as well as externally. But we are not made (or meant to be) that way, are we? Because if we are, then we might as well be manufactured as one would be if they happened to be put together on an assembly line. And then we would all be automatons, or robots; just machines. But we are not.

Derision or simply put, Division

From the moment a body is conceived, it literally begins to die or more formally, reconstruct. And it proceeds in this manner throughout its life, as it continues to develop into a body with substance. Until it reaches its demise, then it is done. In human studies, this is called human maturation. Then once it reaches this formal state of being, it proceeds to disintegrate internally and externally, as if scheduled to. And universally, we call this aging. And either one's body engages in this process slowly, or fairly rapidly; but the end result remains the same for all of us, death. Yet, we are not all hard-wired in the same fashion so we do not age or decay in the same way. Furthermore, we are not automatons either, because if we were, then we would never have to think about age or stages of life; unless, we were pre-programmed to. But either way, even as robots we still might need a complete overhaul just because we have worn out our internal parts; but the outside casing, well that might as well stay the same. That is, unless this external body no longer fit. Then in that case, we would need to figure out what design was better than the old one, right? And then use that as the prototype. But the end result would still be the same: we would never have to think about death or dying, growth or erosion. We were just empty vessels that could be fixed or re-designed now and again to fit the current model whatever that happened to be.

The mind, fortunately, can outgrow its external body. In fact, this was what happened to our earliest ancestors. There were some human forms which evolved into Humanoids, while others remained as they were, as Neanderthals (Battles & Hudak, 2005; Marshack, 1996). And on an evolutionary scale, this meant Man was progressing, growing and evolving too along with Mother Earth. And so, while she was shifting and shaping her environment, we too were adapting to this changing world by shedding our former bodies. We became more than our former selves, animals that lived minute to minute based on our primitive instincts only. We became artisans and tool-makers, crafters and recorders; skilled at some other ways of being than just hunting or fishing, or gathering what the lands had to offer. In essence, we became better. This shift in the environment (and the many that followed), was supposed to mean we were inter-related to her. Environmentally sensitive to Earth and her changes; only it was not Earth per se that made those changes happen, it was also the weather. We could even venture that Mother Nature had a hand in these shifts and that her swings, i.e., seasons, had a greater impact on us than just the Earth erupting from time to time. The eruptions, however, unearthed (no pun intended) how mighty she was, while Mother Nature seemed rather timid in comparison. That is until Mother Nature froze Earth during the Ice Age. Then their contention became suspect. In other words, between these two entities there appeared to be a struggle and Man was caught between them. And as we know, triangulations of this sort never have a winner. But they do have something in common, Man.

In-fighting of this kind seemed, from the earliest of our beginnings, contentious. But why is that? If these two entities, Mother Nature and Earth had issues (and apparently a great deal of them stemmed from their true natures), then how was mankind supposed to know this? Or even align their self with one or the other? Or, even better, not even involve their self in their rivalry? In other words, how does one literally remove their presence from between these two so they can work out their differences? Apparently, this is simply impossible to do, unless we erase an entire race of humans. And to even think we have this kind of power or desire to annihilate a human race, seemed to be the most hideous thought of them all. Yet, as an alternative solution to this kind of war which would never end, it seemed the simplest of answers.

To have this thought, where death was the ultimate solution (to everything) seemed hazardous, to say the least. Because if all we could do is resort to killing, just to dis-entangle ourselves from this ongoing war (which we should never have been party to in the first place), then all we were doing was contributing to the contention. We were not solving anything, just showing how mighty they were, not us. But then, how does one de-triangulate? In other words, how does one become a simpler form? Such as a dyad, or a singleton without destroying the triad? Especially, when we as human beings were not even supposed to be aware of our presence in this war, or that they had chosen to use us as their go-between. But that kind of awareness was also what interfered with communicating directly to one another. So then how were these two huge entities, Mother Nature and Earth supposed to communicate to one another without a human as their receptor and transmitter? Have the animals or other living beings on Earth become these? Then is that not also showing who has the ultimate power? If receptors and transmitters can be exchanged, i.e., where humans are no longer in these two impositions, and animals and other sensate beings are, then is this also not showing who has the upper hand? And that we as humans are no longer needed or necessary for these two impositions. Would that not be wonderful for us? Because then we could focus on what was taking place inside of us, internally. And then once we had us figured out on the inside, then we could turn our attention once again to the outdoors. However, for us to be able to remove ourselves from these two, Earth and Mother Nature, we would also need the mental capacity to know we were doing. Because to do so, also seemed somewhat life-threatening.

We could not imagine first living without Mother Nature because we had become dependent on her for our sustenance. And so to find alternative sources that could sustain us without her input became impossible. However, we could imagine living without Earth and what she provided to us, because we had found alternative solutions to living on her. We could dig into her and live inside of her, as we once did as cave dwellers. We could also climb trees and live in them, as some forest people still do today. We could also build our shelters out of what remained of her, i.e., crafting our houses out of ice or stone or animal pelts or skins, even baking mud into bricks; anything which seemed available to us for our usage: to shelter ourselves and keep us from harm. So not only had we become inter- dependent on Mother Nature because of the food that she provided, but also quite frightened by her as well. Otherwise, why would we need to shelter ourselves? Why not just remain outdoors as we are? But something had shifted. And it was not just that our bodies had altered from that earlier form, we as a species had become aware of her presence, and it was mainly due to the elements.

The power to control the elements was much stronger than what the Earth appeared to produce now and again. In fact, Earth's ability to shake, or erupt every once in a while was dismissed as just what normally takes place when a planet is moving, even gyrating due to the magnetic forces that surround her. So even though Earth was a living organism, just as Mother Nature, she did not cause the same kind of repercussions; and therefore did not garner the same response-set from us. That is we did not need to seek shelter from her when she chose to erupt or shake. And apparently we did not need the air or the ground, or those artifacts which she supplied so we could shelter ourselves. So why did we need Earth? Even more abhorrent was why we should even feel we needed a planet such as Earth at all? What was the purpose for us to be locked onto this planet? Why had she not just spewed us off of her? Or find another means to be rid of us, if we not did hear or feel her in the same way as Mother Nature? Essentially, she could either remove the ozone layer completely, or stop emitting this magnetic force (gravity); which would then theoretically allow us to leave this planet once and for all. Would that not be the best solution for all of us? And then we would not have to make any decisions about ourselves as humans, Earth could make these final decisions for us. But then, why would Earth take this drastic measure with us? But that was just it, was it not? We thought that Earth truly took an interest in us; and even at times, cared. But the harsh reality was she no longer even thought, as if she actually had at one time. Because, truth be told it was just us projecting our thoughts, feelings, even our former beliefs onto her; completely negating Mother Nature. And it was this form of hubris that caused such thoughts to be formulated, and then later discarded. Because once we took away the projections that had been made, i.e., Earth and Mother Nature were these two huge entities, ones that seemed embittered by Man's presence, we could disenfranchise ourselves for this larger system, and virtually disrupt this triangulation, which was just repeating, and repeating and repeating "we humans were only a small part of this larger system." Enough already, we know!

Humans are so stubborn though, they even seem to be genetically engineered to be so. And why is that, do you suppose? Because without this very highly refined stubborn streak (i.e., resilience) the human race would no longer exist. That is force their human existence in-between these two. Remember Earth and Mother Nature happened to coexist a long time without us, then magically, Poof! Humans came into the picture. And lo and behold, these two had to make way for us, did they not? Or else, I wonder would we here at all. But that is beside the point; we are, and because we have this stubborn streak, we have remained here on this planet Earth since that day. Even though it has not been easy, and there are different periods throughout humanity that can attest to this. So, again, would that not seem to be one more indication for why that stubborn streak seems to be due to humans and the way they are encoded? But as we acquired and acclimated to this new found home, we were also increasing this strength, though some might disagree that we should.

Building up stubbornness and resiliency so we could live on this planet, also meant building up our inner and our outer defenses to both of these, not just individually, but as an entire race of humans. And this was not only necessary for expanding ourselves, but also for constructing better homes and shelters, as we too grew on this planet we all call home. However, to do this meant literally moving into other countries, territories both foreign and domestic. Thereby, expanding our kingdoms (as if anyone actually owned this planet and the rights that went along with that); we presumably did, only by an understanding. Yet, this understanding of ours caused quite a stir, did it not? Yes, it did. We not only segmented these lands, into geography; but within these, systems which could stand on their own. Seemingly just to prove who we were; but also to show who held the rights to govern these lands, these kingdoms, even if it was a kingdom of one. But why would one even need to? Especially, if there was only one to really think about.

Lions and Tigers, no Bull

There was, unfortunately, no other conceivable way in which one could prove they were just as stubborn as the next man, without also impeding on their territory. But to take up this endeavor seemed futile too, because all it did was lead to more "in-fighting." Humans fighting among themselves; which is a great distraction from the real world (especially if there is someone or thing watching and finds this entertainment) or as a true escape mechanism, i.e., watching

147

people kill, maim and wound one another just for the fun of watching . But the downfall from all of this was that eventually no one was left to fight; and also no one supposedly left to watch this form of entertainment. And yet fighting amongst ourselves continues to this very day: as a form of entertainment (sport), but also as contentions arise, we still resort to military tactics to convey how stubborn one can be to another human being (military-might and the power supposedly gained just by in-fighting). These two cause even more fights, such as brawls to occur. And when these do, then what made those occur becomes the norm, i.e., what is expected and normal when we are fighting among ourselves.

And you would think, but that has been part of the problem all along, has it not? Thinking had become the mystery, and without it the reason why we still needed to show how stubborn we were (even to ourselves). But that made no sense to us. Especially, when we could simply react; no need for a mind, remember. And no place, apparently to put it either. Because our bodies were pre-formed with everything that one needed, including the most likely place for a mind to be located; and that was in the head, where the brain was located. But our brain seemed incapable (or so it seemed), to hold any other thoughts than the ones that were prescribed in it, such as simple reflections when it was stimulated. That is reacting with the stimulus-response system that we were all born with. However, when we arrived at a certain time in life, historically speaking, we were supposed to know better than to fight; let alone to prove how stubborn one was. Because even though this too was already pre-programmed in us, maybe not the exact moment in time when we would know this; but it was there nevertheless as a part of a very refined part of our survival mechanism. Which is wonderful news for those of us who still feel the need to resort to fighting as a means to entertain oneself, or to prove how stubborn one is; even to resort it as an excuse; we were born with this mechanistic response and not to use it, was such a waste. So why not engage in fighting? Then it makes perfect sense as to why some would still feel the need to fight, even to partake in it plus watch while others prove their self, i.e., how stubborn one could be through this mechanistic stimulus-response technique. Especially, once one learned there were other means to continue this kind of in-fighting, e.g., through one's words or symbols. This way not only could one continue to fight, but one could also engage others in the fight: without having to explain why one was fighting, or that they had been triangulated, i.e., drawn into this form of inter-relating (feuding) without being cognitively aware that they were.

There was a slight discrepancy with this, though. There were those who had no idea there was an ongoing battle, and they had been drawn into it. Secondly, there was also a belief system, one which intentionally drew another into their inter and intra-psychic battles. Because doing so, meant their battles could continue on. But they did this with the knowledge that they were at war with one another. The war zone, though, was supposed to only take place within one's mind, and not on the outside. But once it went outside the limits of one's mind, then it became triangulated with more than just their body and their mind, it literally became a war of the wills. Whose mind was greater, and whose mind would win. And unfortunately, this mind belonged to the leader of a group, and the saddest part of all, it belonged to one family: Narcissus. This one-mind was then supposed to represent one people and one's race. However, the very idea that one needed to fight, and to fight to prove they existed seemed weak and torn directly from a very old world-way of thinking.

By upholding this worldview, though, rather than disputing it only caused more war-like behaviors to co-exist. In other words, leaders whose minds worked in this manner allowed room for their people to be hard-headed, resistant, and destructive all in the name of them. But once this changed, and it no longer was about them; it became a completely different rulership.

Mortal man had taken this room to be who they are literally. They became more stubborn, resistant and destructive, only this time it was about them and not the ruler. Which than meant each individual for themselves, self-governing based on being who they were given the former state of being. Having been accepted, plus the reinforcement for being that way, only made it seem as if they were not only ready to rule their kingdom or the land without a ruler; but they did not need somebody at the top ruling over them. Great news for us humans; we had arrived at a point in time when we no longer needed a ruler, and we could finally govern ourselves based on these highly prized traits alone. No leader, except us.

Combined into this one state of being, though, was not just what one had learned previously was acceptable, but that who had found it to be this way was no longer present. And though this symbolized growth and development in one's human development, the leader who was being emulated was missing knowledge about how to be defiant in a different manner than upholding these three traits, as the best that one could be given the circumstances. They may have known how to be defiant, but not how to surrender or oppose another in an orderly fashion, e.g., deposing their opponent 'limb by limb' without encouragement (in the name of them). So how did one emulate another without also taking on their name? And if one did that, then was one not also becoming just like them? And since we had overturned or usurped our ruler (but not the traits that they approved of), then were we not also headed for disaster? But why would we even think that, *unless* what we just learned to do without – a ruling relationship meant we had become just like them. And yet, was that not the point? Self-governance meant we were supposed to be able to rule just like them; and therefore, we no longer needed them to rule over us. But there was a slight difference between being a follower and then a leader in this form of exchange.

The view from above is different first of all. When one is the leader and has been for many years, only to be overthrown by their people, then it means the followers no longer benefit from their leadership. Or something within them rises up against this form of oppression, and so they take it upon themselves, to make this apparent: by literally taking over the leader's role. And when they do, they not only adhere to what their former leader did, but they also abide by the same rules. So nothing actually changes except the who part, i.e., the human who takes on this leader's position. Nothing ventured, nothing gained. However, there is "gain" made *if* the follower who assumes the leader's position learned something from being in the inferior position. And they are able to refer to this a priori knowledge as they rule. And they can keep both perspectives in mind while ruling.

Is this step-up from a lower position that much different than being born into this position? Yes, actually it is. Because to be able to know that one could be better than their predecessor, meant one had to know their ruler first, inside and out. And also the experience of being less than and inferior to them; and then take this information into consideration. But why would one need to if all they were doing was replacing one leader for another? That made no sense at all. Unless one liked this type of ruling, then one could very well make the case that a solitary leader was all that one land or people could manage at one time. But then we would lose the whole purpose for stepping into a leader's rule after being treated as a peasant or even a non-entity. And that definitely was not going to suffice.

Continuing along this path only seemed to reinforce some of our more basic instincts, such as hunger and sex; which only served to further along what was already known. And it also did nothing but bring forth the bereft (Lopez-Pedraza, 2000). Not only did this form one lethal combination, in reaction to the new ruling regime, but it also seemed to reinforce the non-combatant modality. Wear enough folks down (due to either of these), then not only does that seal one's fate, but ultimately it causes one to suffer too. And in the long run, proving nothing other than one knew how to deflate one's ego; but, also because one knew this, they too could cause further destruction, but choose not to. Now why do you suppose that happened? Especially during a time when one was bereft? Was this what stopped one from becoming "inhuman," or "inhumane" even to another? And if so, why did we not know it then, but we assume to know it now?

Breath

Proving who was either inhumane or inhuman became the next clue into whether or not one was human or not. Now these two choices should not surprise us at this juncture. And why is that? To be thought of as either of these meant *one had to be human*; nothing more, nothing less. But why the choice then? Because to act inhumane and inhuman necessitated the human; but to be considered either of these also meant dampening several aspects of ourselves. It either meant one was not civilized enough to know any better, i.e., childlike, or one never thought about their self as separate from the forest or the land, and therefore held their self in higher regard than another. Or, the worst case scenario, one really did not care that either of these terms were thought of in regards to the human. Mainly due to their past ties to the Animal Kingdom, and this form of life; ergo they were also seen or appeared to be misfits (only partially aware of what it means to act inhuman or inhumane, according to our current understanding of what it means to be fully human). But living only partially aware of how these ways of being were collapsed into one body or into one mind, also caused greater disturbances out there. Why would that be, though, especially if one was quite comfortable knowing that both of these existed in one form or another inside of these? But was that not it? We had thought we did not mind having these housed in a human body, but we erred on the side of "just being human" too many times. And this resulted in too many feudal wars, and more importantly, feudal warlords.

But feuds and warlords were to be expected were they not? They were a part of our legacy as living human beings. Even as living legacies, though, these types of human relationships and relational styles at some point in time were supposed to stop. And preferably before they became known as the only way to be in this life, i.e., as a feudal warlord who lived to see another day only so they could fight. And if they could not find a worthy opponent, they fought in their head, literally. Strategizing, and finding common ground on which to do battle. And this way not only could one see their way through a fight, fighting as only a warrior would; but they also could laud over their wins, and even downplay (if not completely ignore) their losses. Thus increasing in their mind's eye their power and their strength, but also glorifying this inner kingdom. This only became "a nuisance" when it became the only way to act, and behave in this man's world.

At some point in time, however, we were supposed to be beyond these. No longer egotistical or self-centered, Man was also supposed to be beyond mentally stimulating his or her self through engineering a fight or two. Even if it happened to be just within one's conscience as they strategized. So for example, how many men will I lose if I engage in this battle, but not in that one? Or, if I choose to engage in a war, what will happen to me as their leader? Will I be seen for my heroics rather than as a tyrant? And would that not assist me to be a better fighter and leader? And therefore, not only justify the need for war, but to war. And even more importantly, by engaging in these kinds of tactics, one could also increase their significance in this world with their home winnings, such as bringing home the opponent's head even if it happened to once be one's family member. And was that not a sight to see! No, not really. Seeing it though was also a warning to others who even thought they had a chance to dethrone this ruler. And the fact that it was a head from a kinsman only reinforced this.

This form of rulership used decapitation, as if it were the only tactic to prove who was in charge. And they would continue to rule in this manner and use this form of control no matter the cost. In these families' structure, the need for control over-ruled all. There was no convincing them otherwise, and there was also no room to think otherwise too. This form of ruling was literally "ruling with an Iron Fist," and there was no diverting from this. However, it did not mean that one did not try to change this, knowing that when they attempted to, they would pay either with their head or another family member's.

Unfortunately, this form of rulership also drew attention to the very thing one abhorred the most, loss. Plain and simple, one did not like to lose. This much obstinance in both directions, the subject's and the ruler's not only perpetuated the end result, a loss of one's head; but also the same result time after time: The subject losing. Until one fine day, it was the ruler who lost his head. Then no longer was he in charge. But that did not necessarily mean the "new" ruler was any better than the former one. Or did it? If one was smarter than they, because they had succeeded where no other before them had (by decapitating their ruler), then did that not make them the better ruler? Yes and no. Yes, because obviously they had been able to kill this ruler. And they displayed his head as a way to show who the new boss was.

But did that not also mean by the time that they had decapitated him, they too had learned a thing or two about deceit. Because to overthrow one's ruler and to decapitate him, also meant the subject had to be better at killing than their former leader. Now why might that be?

Losing one's head strictly for power and control made no sense at all. But it did, if one felt like they could not control their self or their body (their people) without some form of unusual punishment. And it just happened to be by taking a head and "trophy-ing" it. But did it have to be in the form of taking the head of a family member? Yes. Because at this time, there were not that many people who were not blood-related. So "accidentally" severing the head from their opponent's body, not only signified Death to the next individual who stepped out of line, or chose to do battle with this family; but that if they chose not to, they were thought of as cowardly. This injury then became the center of attention, not the argument or the reason the battle began with. This was a personal offense; the first of its kind. And once that was acknowledged, then whoever made that injury appear became the target.

As we know there are battle scars, and then there are battles which should never result in anyone being injured. Even in one's family system. But, occasionally when fights get out of hand or are even instigated (encouraged) to show who is the most powerful one of all, then collateral damage is to be expected. Right? But hand to hand combat which resulted in a physical injury was not tolerated if it resulted in dismemberment. That seemed too extreme unless one was making that a point, i.e., one did indeed need their hand or their foot, even their head if they had plans to lead their men into a battle. But if that was what they were destined to be, a warrior with a cause, and they had lost these while "in-training" and furthermore, within this family system; then not only did that signify dishonor, but also no affinity to war. In other words, to lose either of these limbs was better than learning to defend oneself the right way. But that was just it? Was one not in-training to learn what "the right way" was? And was this not also the best way to train somebody to fight, by injuring them even if it meant they had to lose a hand or a foot? And was this also not the best way to teach a fighter? That these types of injuries were the natural result of learning how to fight; but, when one was just learning how to fight and they happened to lose a body part through this endeavor; then there was more than just, learning how to fight the right way that was at stake. Somebody had taken their power too seriously, and had used it abusively. And why is that assumed here, when all we are doing is talking about the past and the natural outcome of learning to do battle with another inside of one's family?

Dismembering another while in training to be a fighter should never happen, unless that was the only way one could succeed. In either dispensing with one's enemy (even if it happened to be one's brother) or, it just happened to be the only way one could formally act out that they did not want to be a warrior. And that possibly, they never were meant to be. And the only way that this could be shown was in their mortal actions. Through injuring one while they were in training. This not only solidified that they could mortally wound another, but that they did not stop at just cutting off a limb, i.e., randomly, but chose a specific area of the body to hone in on. For example, to cut-off a hand completely not only disfigured the body, but also kept their opponent from being able to pick up a sword in that hand ever again. And the foot, well that one is actually even easier to hone in on. If one no longer had a foot to stand on, well...get my drift?

This only worked if the "victor" happened to be the one who still held their sword in the hand that was still attached to their body. But this did not hold true, if they lost their foot; for if they could no long stand on two feet, then not only were they crippled; but they were literally no longer able to take that stance again, i.e., they no longer could attain the title of a swordsman. And, once that happened, then they also were no longer able to fight using this kind of weapon. But that did not rule-out learning how to fight using another means, such as a gun or a rifle. Some other alternative method for killing or maiming another just so one could prove who: either the better fighter was, or who knew how to kill and maim another. Even if it happened to be one's brother; and that was the point.

Obfuscation

This, though, seemed entirely senseless even to the most rationale of minds. And why was that? After they had displayed their brawn through these types of actions, would it not be enough just to see that one could sever a limb? But apparently not. For one, seeing one's might every day only reinforced that one had (or held) that kind of power in their hands. And secondly, because one could deal a blow that severed a body part, then why not press it? That is, why not see if one could strengthen their agility by fighting someone who was stronger and more powerful? And that way, not only would that prove how capable one was as a swordsman, but also in the process prove they were born to wield a sword. Would this not be the best way to take care of the problem? But, this kind of in-home training (fighting) was not the source of the problem. It only appeared to be when it was taken out of one's home, and into a larger environment. Then it became more than just learning how to be a better swordsman, one actually held "lethality" in one's hands.

To wield that kind of power, even temporarily seemed magical even gratifying, which also led one to be thought of as insensitive and vulgar. Perhaps also that they had been groomed to be a highly skilled fighting machine, which only knew how to use one weapon, a sword; but this was enough to prove and fulfill one's destiny. One was basically following in the footsteps of another fighting machine; thus, not only fulfilling one's legacy, but perhaps improving on the legend bequeathed to them. But what was that exactly? Was one supposed to draw one's sword each and every time one felt the need to? Perhaps, not.

Perhaps, one was supposed to know who the enemy was before they actually drew their sword. Or at least be wary of drawing it too quickly or too often just because they had been finely tuned to react as a fighting machine. But that too was a part of what happened through this formal training process. One literally became better at fighting (i.e., brawling); and the more one perfected this technique, the better one became at it. They became better at drawing their sword, wielding it, and then using it to sever a body part from their opponent. But they also became quicker and better at this, each and every time they repeated this same maneuver over and over again; till it literally became just another reflex. Draw a sword, "fight" for a few seconds, but then sever their opponent's hand or their foot from their body, and then stop. Replace the sword or just walk away, leaving them there: Body parts and all. Or, perhaps extinguish their life now and again. That would be an improvement would it not? Rather than leaving them there, wounded. Then not only was one killing their enemy every once and a while, but this maneuver would also surprise their enemy. That this individual known for their brawn only, would go in for the kill; because that took more than just severing a hand or two, or even a few feet.

Killing and not just injuring another, led one to believe they were a killing machine, and not just a fighting machine. They could literally *take* another's life. And this led one into believing they were the most powerful one on Earth. And this thought and the action not only led to more than just wielding a sword, and using it to show how powerful one had become (or was already); but it also proved beyond a shadow of a doubt, strength.

If one could just maim their opponent, then one could predict the outcome: one was going to lose a limb when encountering this kind of fighting machine. But once a life was taken by the sword of this same individual, then not only did they become even more lethal than they were before, i.e., when they unsheathed their sword, one was certain they would lose a hand or a foot. But now one did not know for sure that when there was a "fight," they were going to lose their life in place of losing either of these. And yet, it was better to know one would be crippled for life after fighting this individual, then to literally lose one's life unexpectedly. But that was just it, was it not? Fighting of any kind typically resulted in loss. But now the stakes were raised to include "life."

Losing one's life to this kind of individual was surprising, and then it was demeaning. If not downright degrading. And why might that be? Because they were the idiot; they just picked up their sword "fought" then severed one's hand or foot. There literally was no finesse to them. But there lay the fallacy. We thought as their opponent there was more to them than just their being a fighting machine. But when they took a life for the very first time, it not only surprised us, it literally showed they were more than this. Then, not only did that action relegate them to a different position, it looked to be a skill they had developed; rather than what it simply was, an accident. And they happened to have killed another. However, it was not an accident at all. The hand that lifted up that sword and thrust it into the body had made it very clear they were going for the kill. And why was that? Because the other two areas were peripheral locations; whereas, thrusting a sword into the mainframe, i.e., the body of one's enemy, literally meant death. And it was intended that way for a reason.

For one, "brute strength" no longer was recognized as something to acquire or aspire to. Especially, if it only entailed taking a hand or a foot from another, and there really was no fighting involved; it was, however, one of the basest ways to fight. And to show one's strength; but one which only seemed to reinforce the brute, and not the art of sword fighting. But by being seen as brutish, rather than a half-wit or as a primitive being, meant they were more than either of these. Based solely by one's actions, even if they were only reacting on impulse, or had been trained to react that way, i.e., to pick-up a sword and cut-off another's body parts. In the name of continuing on this kind of tradition, which was apparently putting down another, even if it was just to prove one's strength. But when this self-same individual took the initiative, and proceeded to slay their fighting partner, then, not only were they doing so of their own accord, *but* they were making an alternative choice in the face of what was known about them. This type of individual was formally known to only cut-off one's hand or one's foot, but not to take a life. And to do so now (not in the literal sense of this word), meant something had triggered inside of them. And the end result of that was death. But to die by this individual's sword? There literally was no dignity in it. There was only brutality, nothing more, nothing less.

When the only reason to pick up a sword was to slice off a hand or a foot, without more than just a few seconds of "dueling," then not only was there no point to the fighting (other than to show that one could) but to engage in a fight like this, also seemed completely pointless. Unless, one only wanted to have the certainty that their hand or their foot would be taken; then it became who's hand or foot would be lost. And then once this was decided, then they had "won it" fair and square. But then these became the trophy markers; i.e., the sign to end it all, no hand or no foot, and therefore, no need to continue to fight. But when that happened it demonstrated nothing but one could do this; it showed nothing in the way of rulership or even desiring to be in power (or even in charge). That is until one killed. Then, killing and taking another's life showed initiation, but only if one had forgotten the lesson. To be in power, especially in this man's world, meant one had to kill at some point, and they had to be able to cut-off their opponent's head. And they had to show it. This then was supposed to prove beyond a shadow of doubt: who that individual was, and what family they originated from. And their ability to kill and return with the head was supposed to prove they could rule just like their predecessors. But it only became problematic if one took too many heads, or they happened to use this very same technique to kill their former ruler. Because this then set precedence: If one ruler could overthrow another through decapitating them, or prove how powerful they were through decapitation alone (and it did not matter whose head or how many were taken), then why not just use these "rules" as the sole justification for one's actions? But also to solidify this was supposed to be how one ruled, because this was how one was brought up to be. And that was to be a tyrant who went on tirades, which resulted in slaughter and ruin, which supposedly proved how powerful they were. And by extension, this was the way one ruled their people, but not by solely killing them. They were supposed to also be governing their people through decapitation too; and not just doing away with their enemy through this manner too. But that was again a sign that war and punishment did mix well when one was also supposed to be an abomination.

One abomination was most certainly supposed to be enough to end all the feuds and the wars, unless that is what they were supposed to do, bring a reign of terror that never, ever ended. But it should have stopped when the madness became a bloodbath. Because even to this day, we still have rulers who govern their people through decapitation, and proving their strength and how powerful they are, through this form of coercion. But then it becomes, believe it or not, a battle of the wills. While one is off beheading another, i.e., ruling their land in this manner, there are others who are plotting to do the same to them. Which is one way to model this kind of behavior: kill the oppressor and this reinforces how it is supposed to be done. And by doing that, also reinforcing that decapitating another is the only way to rule; and by that also sealing one's fate: one must also be ready to be beheaded too. But then, at this point in our history, it did not matter who was king or queen if any insubordination of any kind was intolerable or led to death. In other words, it did not matter who was one at that time "death by beheading" was the common rule, and the only means to settle a feud or a simple argument.

So this meant no matter whom one was or thought they would like to become, a king or the ruling party, there simply was no alternative but resigning oneself to this fate. They were pre-destined to lose their head once they became the ruler. And they knew this. So then this became foretelling: once they became the ruler, then they knew what was in store for them. And while they ruled they knew this fate. And it hung over them as a truth. But knowing that this was one's chosen fate; would one not also attempt to change it once they were in power? And would this not be their first decree, to abolish this form of assassination forthwith? Because if they did not, then they would not rule for very long; however, if one truly believed in this fate (they became king or queen through this method of killing and that was how it was meant to be), then so be it. No need to change anything or to be frightened away from ruling or being a ruler, it was all foretold to be this way. However, they could also opt to keep this truth going knowing what was indeed in store for them: Rule and eventually you will lose your life too through decapitation. So then, why not also recognize this could also serve to be a form of punishment if one tried to rule before they were supposed to or were meant to. And this worked. As long as they were the ruling party, they could use this technique to enforce their legacy. In other words, the family one was born into was also supposed to be the only ruling family and they were supposed to be for centuries. And so, then could justify their actions by in-killing family members when need be. And thereby signify their rulership.

Using death to become the next ruler was then transformed into a punitive means to lord over one's land. But to take this "inheritance" out of what was already known among one's family, and into the open market meant one had to know they were *the* authority and death was their accomplice. And they would demonstrate this by showing it. This meant demonstrating this relationship out in public, pure and simple. They then had to find someone they could use to prove how this punitive method worked. Which literally meant they had to seek out someone (other than a family member) that they could kill, and they had to behead that someone; bringing them to their death through beheading them. But to make this a form of punishment, they had to perform this feat out in the open, and in front of a large audience; otherwise, no one would believe this individual was capable of killing someone else besides their own; and that they had beheaded them.

But why the spectacle? Why the need for this demonstration of power to be brought out into the public's eye? So it could literally be transformed into a form of punishment, and not just utilized as a transference of power that also garnered the prestige of having done so. So then by taking it out doors into a public arena, not only was this ruler stepping outside of what was commonly known on the inside; but by doing so, they were increasing their power exponentially. When this individual made the decision to demonstrate their technique outside and in front of a group of people, they were literally disclosing their ritual. And when they did this "disclosure," in front of an audience, they were showing what they had done to accomplish their rise to power. However, for this to become a form of punishment in the public's eye (and not just a way to rise to this position of rulership), one had to make a decree, and make it stick. And the best way to accomplish this was to take matters into one's hand: Go out and perform this in front of a group of people. Then supplement this action with the words, i.e., the decree: That if anyone considers disobeying their ruler, they will be punished by losing their head. This then not only reinforced the action, i.e., this is what it looks like to lose one's head (in plain sight), but it also solidified the power of one man's actions. Yet their words, along with taking another man's head and their life, just to inform them this was going to be their punishment for disobeying them? That took more than just "airing out one's dirty laundry," it meant that one either had a guilty conscience or they were being visited by someone from their distant past who told them to, go out and inform the masses of what had been done. Then use it as a form of punishment, a formal one.

Apparently this type of governance was not ruling alone. That then meant they had an accomplice (and it was Death). Announcing this out in the public domain, though, seemed strange; even abnormal. Beyond what was even called for. Everyone knew Death. And they knew it from living day to day, even moment to moment. But the need to make it a form of punishment, seemed lurid and unbelievable. Why would one seek Death out and form a relationship with it? And then turn around and use their relationship formally, as a form punishment? Especially, if everyone was already familiar with death, and knew what it looked like? So what was the purpose for imposing death on those who already knew they would die? If they recognized death as the final

171

moment of life, then this form of punishment would neither instill death as a fear, nor would it be see as much of a threat. It would just be considered as another part of living and then dying. Happens every day, right? *But*, because it was their relationship (the one the family had with Death) that was being demonstrated out in public, it was also very powerful. It not only showed the public one could summon Death within a moment's notice; but by being able to do so, they were showing they could, which was quite different than just watching "death" take place normally. This then not only solidified their personal relationship with Death, but it also took the mystery out of how they became the ruler. It also showed who they were aligned with, and it certainly was not with Life. But it may also be that having to go out and perform this ritual in front of an audience had more to do with the mortal than with either Life or Death.

Performing this death scene out in the open, so that others could see exactly what it took to become this kind of ruler, also made this technique known to the outside in the form of a punishment. And it was supposed to do so, to show the power this ruler held so that they could rule without disobedience. Thus by going out and demonstrating this method to the public, they were also showing how powerful they were, and that they were not afraid to carry-out this deed in the form of a punishment. Once it was demonstrated to them, then the people knew that they would be punished. And it might be their ruler who beheaded them (but more than likely not). Why? Because plain and simple they were no longer needed as the one to wield the sword. Once this demonstration was over, and they made their decree known through their words, then the enactment of this ritual into power was semi-completed. Because then the next step literally was for someone to disobey them. Otherwise, why the need to demonstrate this ritual act out in public? Because, they were doing exactly as they were told to do. But by being this explicit in their actions, they were not only proving their self as a ruler, but upholding their loyalty. But it was not to the family as one would expect; it was to Death.

Death was known to all at this time. The ruler and their people lived with it and Life constantly. But what they did not know was that this ruler was now taking a family rite of passage out into the public's eye. And, because they did not know of this intention, they also did not know presumably, who informed this leader to do so. And furthermore, why they found it necessary to re-enact this particular rite of passage in front of them? What was the purpose for this kind of disclosure? So that they could formally acknowledge their allegiance to Death, and pledge to uphold his doctrine; and not another's.

Death, by virtue of its very presence (along with Life) was everywhere. And because of this, they did not seem to need this kind of demonstrative action. Unless, there was an imbalance of power along with the prestige of knowing who ruled better than the other. But to take this "imbalance" out into the open seemed rather out of the question. And why was that? Because, all one had to do was take a good look at their surroundings, and know who lived with Death, and who lived with Life. Therefore, there was no need to demonstrate or form an alliance with either of them. In fact, one could live in this neutral space, and never give either of them another thought. But that was not acceptable. One was not allowed to remain neutral or to go on living without recognizing them. So that meant one had to choose, Death, Life or neutrality. And, as I mentioned earlier, one had. One had chosen Death to partner with, not Life. But by making this their obvious choice, did that also mean Life was the loser? It did. But it did in the most unusual fashion.

Since Life was not chosen, then it was left with no other alternative but to go on as is. Life unpartnered not only meant unencumbered by Death, i.e., she could go on indefinitely, but she could do so without anything or anybody. Eternal: No body, no thing to be attached to; therefore, forever free as a spirit should be. And Life was aware of this. She knew she was better off than Death

because he was bound to the physical, and freedom was not
an option; poor fellow. He was attached to a need. He
needed a body for his presence to be known. But why was he
any different than her? He, too, was a spiritual presence. Yet,
for him to need to be embodied just so he could be seen, not
only seemed out of the ordinary; it seemed strange. And
what was even stranger was that a mortal would choose him.
But Life had literally left this option out. There was no
choosing with her, only with him. That was what was so
unique about Death. He necessitated the choice. But he also
needed; and that was the major difference between him and
Life; so when he paired with a mortal being, choice and his
need were both made transparent. As long as there were
mortals willing to choose him, and recognize his need for
them; then he could go on living in their bodies, making his
presence known to them. Death could then walk among the
living, and we would think nothing of it. We knew we were
mortal beings, who were also time limited, did we not? And
so by making our choice to be with him transparent, we were
demonstrating we knew this and we knew it through him. To
be with him, meant certain death.

Living with this knowledge and with Death, though, also
showed a sense of maturity. One which came with age, and
also in the re-telling; one knew they were mortal and they
were going to die. And lastly, they knew how, by Death. But

they also knew that each one of them embodied him, within this family system; which also meant they knew how they were going to meet Him at the end: through decapitation. This was common knowledge among those who chose to know Death way back when. But to uphold the religious side, i.e., the belief that the only way to become the next ruler one had to officiate it, by cutting off the head of their former ruler-leader; meant one not only believed they should be the next ruler, but they also believed in Death. And they complied. This then became a custom.

After having experienced this once in one's lifetime, it was enough to prove that Death reigned over Man. It was the deed, the beheading of a family member that signified they were one. Because if one could kill their ruler, i.e., the head of the family, just to prove they were ready to rule; then that was enough to form the oath, the pact with Death. But it also showed the others who was ascending to the throne as the next ruler, Man but with Death alongside him. And each time this was re-enacted, they together became much more powerful; till eventually one grew accustomed to knowing this was so. But this was their lineage, not one that everyone took upon their self to follow. And thankfully so.

Who would want to behead a family member just so that they could rule their way? And secondly, were there no other choices other than taking the life of this elder, so that one could rule within this same family? And lastly, was their no affection within this family system? Because it would seem that if this was there, then they would not use beheading their ruler, as the only way to ascend. But apparently there was no affection and there was no thought given to killing, possibly even to beheading. Because by severing one's head from the body, one was not only showing their might, i.e., how tough they were, but they were also intentionally dismembering the trunk from the head: Thus claiming that when these two parts were no longer together, Death was all the more present. But in addition, without the head and body together, one was not whole and one was not a life anymore; and without either of these, then not only was the feat accompli, Death was no longer needed. So he could by all rights go on his merry way. But he chose not to in this particular family line. In fact, after each death, he grew in strength. And the more strength that he drew through the re-enactment of their wishes, the greater his presence became known to them. And the greater he became, so did they just by the mere fact they embraced him too; because after each enactment, they learned what they had done in that enactment, they had taken a given life. Which was much different than going outside of one's home, and taking another's head; because once one did that, they were no longer thought to be a part of this family's lineage or their legacy.

Dealings with this particular family not only included Death, but knowing he was with them as a constant. So if one was to conduct any business transactions with this family, there was no reason to suspect one's life was in danger. In fact, as an outsider one was comforted in knowing they were not in danger of losing their head or their life to this family; because that was the ruling party's arrangement with Death. And as an outsider, if the ruling family's succession depended on this arrangement with Death; then so be it. However, once this knowledge became common, i.e., that one would not lose their life or be decapitated because they were not a part of the ruling class, and they were just doing business as usual with this family; then something changed. What though? What made this kind of arrangement with Death unacceptable? Obviously, when exchanging one head for another was just this family's rite of passage, there were no questions about why this was done. It was normal inside this family's system. However, once that ruler broke from their family's way of doing business with Death, and it became public knowledge that beheading one's family member was the way they had become the ruler, and it also became the way one would now be punished as an outsider; then there was nothing one could do to alter this lineage. They were the rulers and they were the ones with the most power, right? Yet, just because this ruler made it known that this was the way in which their family had grown in stature, it did not mean that was the only way Death grew.

Death "needed" and because he did, he was the one who pressed people (and especially this family in particular) to bring him on before it was their time. But how was one to know it was their time if one was not a part of this rulership? They had refined knowledge; and with it, they knew when Death needed to make his appearance known to them. And they knew this by knowing when it was time for a new leader. But once this no longer applied, i.e., one had taken the means out of the family, and applied (or hoped to) to the outsiders, then Death lost his power to rule only over this family. In fact, when this ruler went outside the family, and demonstrated how Death was done, the ruler gained two-fold: one, he broke the cardinal rule never to disclose what took place behind closed doors; and secondly, by doing so, he had formed a stronger allegiance to Death, and weakened considerably his mortal side. Because anyone who was willing to demonstrate how to behead another without good reason (i.e., except for replacing one ruler with another) was out of their mind literally. And yet, Death was this not also Death's doings?

He, too, was a part of this ruler's mind. And so for them both to make a fundamental decision (a dissolution with this particular family) by choosing to go out among the masses,

179

and show them what they could do together, (i.e., as the ruler
– mortal with Death) not only seemed to be out of the
ordinary; but, abnormal at the same time. That is, why would
they both need to enact this rite of passage out in the open?
In front of strangers, those who were outside their family?
There must have been a reason for this kind of action to take
place, outside. For one, by displaying their power in a
completely different arena, i.e., in front of others who were
not in their family system, they were disclosing their power
together. They could take another individual and behead
them. And then this was supposed to show them: One, who
held the most power; and two, what would happen if they
transgressed them. But then, how was one to know which
rule brought beheading to the individual who was not a part
of this family? Plain and simple betrayal.

When this method was demonstrated out in public, it was
then made clearer still by the words that were uttered by this
particular ruler: whoever disobeys me, will lose their head.
And now that you know that, be forewarned. But was this
not also a part of their legacy? That is, in this ruling family
they had been taught that someday they too would
eventually behead, and also lose theirs at some point too.
And this was foretold, i.e., what fated them. Yet, when this
ruler-mortal along with Death went out into the public
domain with their technique, showed and announced what

they intended to do if disobeyed; then not only were they subjecting the audience, i.e., making it very clear they were now the subjects, but they were also making a statement: They were in power. And they intended to make sure it remained that way. But whoever heard of wanting to remain in power forever? And that they had to make this very forthright statement so that all knew it? And lastly, why use the method of beheading to prove this point? To prove that they not only wanted to rule forever, but they were *the* mightiest ruler to date. And to make that plain, all one had to do was take what they knew out of this family's system of rulership, and present it to their people.

Breaking from this family's bloodline by performing this ritual act outside, not only drew attention to this particular individual ruler, making him the center of attention, but it also brought him something else, status: The social kind. But this should have been "a given." That is, he should have by birthright been recognized by the people as the rightful heir and ruler. And they should have held him in deference just because of this. And they did. But when he went out intentionally, to show and to tell the public about how he was going to rule them, through disobedience and punishment, then he was also differentiating himself from all the former rulers. And he was acknowledging this to himself, his family and to the public. And by doing that, he was essentially establishing himself as the new ruler, and also making a name for himself; which also meant he was not just looking to break free of his family's name or their bloodline, but to standout, above all the rest. To do this though, meant taking what he knew, and using it to distinguish his rulership.

The maniacal partner, Death, who happened to be the invisible essence in this mortal-spirit partnership, seemed non-present. And it was not until this was shown, i.e., what they could do together by beheading another who was not a part of the family's bloodline that it finally "hit home" what kind of rulership they were under: an Egomaniac's. Now why would it take an exhibition of this kind, to prove how diabolical this form of rulership was? Because if they had not taken an outsider and beheaded them; and showed that they could, all they would be doing was demonstrating what was already known or suspected about this family. They could behead and they too knew about Death. But they broke through the collusion, by taking a complete stranger and beheading them out in public; decrying that if anyone under their rule broke ranks, they too would lose their head and their body; but not to Death. This time they would lose it for betraying this ruler.

Funny (not really); okay, ironic then that the one whose family encouraged their people to be just like them "back in the day" now found this to be intolerable. Earlier there were three basic characteristics which were acceptable. And they were: belligerence, defiance, and equal competition for whatever spoils happened to be out there. Each of these characteristics was a part of being mortal; and as long as they were housed within a human body, and kept alive this way; then the behaviors associated to them were also permitted to be exhibited. With one caveat, *the people could demonstrate these three characteristics, as long as they did so under this ruling party's name.* However, when this was no longer understood, there was nothing for this ruler to do, but conceive of another way to rule his people (if he so chose to). This was a part of this family's legacy; they went from one externalization to basically, nothing. Would that not confuse most people? Apparently not; when this kind of covert message was "delivered and understood," there literally was no need to micromanage the people or their behaviors, because they were sanctified. The ruler was doing these so I could too; and therefore, no responsibilities whatsoever. And even better still, nothing to worry about, except for those gosh, darn outsiders. And those few who either did not adhere to this informal doctrine, or just happened not to abide by the rules of this "lord," but they still happened to occupy the same territory as this man's rulership.

The means for succeeding to the throne through beheading was literally taken away from this ruling family, once it was demonstrated out in the open by one of their own. Because once it was, then, this assured that the family's succession method was no longer a secret. And this ruler chose to show it, rather than just tell his people what his family had done. Taking the initiative to make this method and this family's secret known, though, also shifted his place in the family; actually, it tore him completely away from this ruling family and their values. But, even though he chose to make this drastic move away from them, he was also announcing to them, i.e., the people, he no longer desired to be a part of the family or their system. Thus, not only singling out who he was: an individual who no longer held this particular secret in the family; but he was also informing the public of this truth. Thereby, not only acknowledging they were no longer ruling him, i.e., the family, but that he alone had chosen to bring their secret out into the public domain for all to see. No one else would defy the legacy, or Death, until he did.

Until this ruler disclosed their succession method out in the open, this family and their secret remained safely kept within this family's peculiar system of ascension. Which should have been fine, as long they were the rulers; but once this ruler took the initiative, by displaying their succession rite out in the open, then, not only was he making what they knew transparent, but he literally changed it. Instead of it being a rite of passage into a new life, it was a method of delivery into a new world; where death and dismemberment were permitted. In fact, they were the expected. If one lives in a harsh world, such as what life was primarily supposed to be like back when this form of rulership was in power; then, naturally death was to be expected. But not, dismemberment; this was a method. And it was supposed to show how gruesome (or powerful) one was in their interactions with another. That is until this ruler took this out from under his people, and showed them how this family had killed their former rulers. And then this method of dismembering another not only became cruel, but it was there and then when it became punishment.

But losing one's head, this one body part was nothing compared to losing one's hand or one's foot. Because "death" was certain when one was beheaded, but, this did not hold true when one lost their hand or their foot in a battle, or while learning to fight; that was disgraceful. However, they did hold one similarity in common with beheading another; they were disobedient. And either this was because they had not followed the rules as they were instructed to, or they had. But the end result all looked the same: one's body was not whole anymore. And that supposedly killed the spiritual agreement with this particular mortal; but it had not. Remember this agreement only held true, once the head was dismembered from the body. There was nothing mentioned about losing other body parts while doing battle with another; or, even while learning how to. In fact, this was when Death probably felt slighted. And that was when he sought justice. But if there is no formal agreement between this spirit and the human who has lost a hand or a foot, then how could Death seek justice? Or even deem he needed to? Especially, if he needed a whole body, and not a partial one?

So who would be crazy enough to link-up with Death, if that was his demand? Man did; and he did so for one reason only apparently, so that we would not continue to live life indefinitely. The mortal side of us somehow knew that we needed this ultimate decision made for us. And in this peculiar family and their understanding of the very first agreement that they made with Death, they took him literally at his word. Death wanted whole bodies, not partial ones. And he wanted them to remain that way, until he needed to depart. Then he called upon the mortal to make him happen. And in this family of warlords, beheading was his way of dissolving and re-instating himself in this family. But outside of these people, he reigned differently. Did he not? He "died" along with them. And his escape went unnoticed a majority of the time. They were just cadavers, bodies stiffened through his process of decay. However, if they chose this form of living with Death, this would keep the body whole, and for some this was preferred over decapitation any day. But it meant living and dying slowly, naturally or diseased. The dismemberment of the body, other than how it was ordained by Death, voided all deals with him. What a relief, sort of?

At least if one was a warlord in this particular family, one knew that Death was eminent. And when it happened, Death would make one's death quick and clean. This was a better alternative than living unrecognized, maimed, or dying in disgrace, e.g., after exsanguination was brought on due to losing one's hand or one's foot through a fight. But also by choosing to align oneself to Death, one's nobility was understood. And it was to remain that way. Agreeing to be with him was supposed to mean no one else was supposed to know this method. And it was supposed to be kept behind closed doors, between immediate family members only. That is until the incident. When their ruler went against his family, and took their rite of passage out into the open, then not only did he change their legacy; but, it no longer was "noble" to behead. The act itself was lessened by the very fact that it was shown to outsiders.

Once this ruler made the decision to expose the family out in the public domain, then it also shifted the family's dynamics. They had agreed that they were to be the rulers and how that happened was to remain inclusive, knowledge that only their family knew. However, by having taken their sacred rite out into the open, and demonstrating it, this ruler was intentionally breaking this formal agreement. The ruler had shown what they had been doing; and along with that, made a decree that if anyone disobeyed him, then their head would be taken. Which was supposed to bring people to the realization that this ruler meant business; and not to listen, or obey him, meant being beheaded.

Demonstrating this family's secret and their rite was incomprehensible. How could one take what they had known for years out into the public eye? And then live with the knowledge that they had just betrayed their family by doing so? By the time this individual came to rule, there was no family to speak of. They had become meaningless even more than they were originally. Now, though, they were just a group who happened to cohabit a dwelling. And it was one that was made fit for a king or a queen to live in; but only one of these could rule at one time. That was the autocratic way. Which then meant when an heir apparent was coming of age, in this family, it was their time to rule and they had to behead whoever happened to be the ruler; and it did not matter, male or female. There was no gender bias in this family. Yet, what this ruler wanted, sole power and the authority which came from this family, was not enough. This ruler in particular needed to make public what was already known to this family, and to do so in the only way they knew how, make a spectacle: A public display. Thereby proving to the family (which really no longer existed) they no longer held the power, or the authority to determine when he or she should abdicate their rulership. Once this was formally acknowledged by way of this open and very public demonstration, then by all rights nobody governed anybody, if only for an instant; but that was all it took.

When the ruler took their rite of passage and used it in a sanctimonious way, there was just a second for Death to appear and then disappear, as he normally would. However, there was "no other" for Death to enter, so he had to return to the ruler making the demonstration. And because there was no other place for him to go but back to the family member who was performing this ritual, Death was being defied. But also by having to return to this ruler's head, it caused them both to become fused even more than they were before. He thought that in this enactment he was being summoned as agreed upon, but when he emerged and saw that this was not so; and he had to return to that ruler's head rather than another, then no wonder Death was baffled. But only for a moment; once he realized what that performance was for: to demonstrate how powerful he was; then it no longer mattered that he had been called forth, and subsequently returned. Both of which happened within a moment's notice. It was the performance of the method, which was being dignified, signified in a completely different manner than how it had once been known as a ritual enactment: sacred and prescribed. Now that this ritual was performed out in public, it lost it secrecy (which was the most potent part of the enactment of it). As long as it was held in secret, it could by virtue of this alone, continue anointing others within this so called family. But once it became common, and prohibitive, i.e., to be used only for punishing those who disobeyed them; then it became formulized. And, presumably, it did not matter who did the beheading. As long as it was known who they were disobeying. This proclamation "righted" what had apparently been lost, during a time when attention to details was just taking off.

Fine or "gross" motoric skill building

Death was their spirit. But because he was theirs and he had no other choice but to remain so,   no one actually saw Death move out of this ruler's head, or return to it. This all transpired without anybody's knowledge but Death's. Entrapping himself once again in this ruler's head, only this time, informed "differently." Having no other choice, but to return to this particular ruler, meant he was no longer acknowledged as he once was. And the only ones who knew this were Death and this ruler. This ruler was for all intents and purposes, defaming them. The ones who by birthright took a solemn oath to abide by Death's wish; and Death, who initially gave these individuals no other recourse, but to obey him or else. However, while Death was summoned repeatedly through their re-enactment rite, Death was "robbed" of this opportunity when this ruler made the choice to behead another: One that was not a part of this inclusive group. Thus, disobeying everything (or so it seemed) that this grouping held sacred.

When Death was freed, he was not. In actuality, the enacting of this sacred rite in front of the people was nothing but a "set-up," a staged production for the public to see what this family had done; it was not an actualization of their transferring one's power and authority to the heir apparent. But that display fooled Death. He literally thought that when this ruler chose to behead that other, he was moving into the next ruler's body; but he was not. In fact that was when Death was confused. For one, no other mortal being had done that before: taken this sacred rite out into the public for all to see him. And secondly, since he (the mortal being) failed to follow through with this special rite of passage, Death never went outside of that ruler's mind and into the other autocrat. And the reason for that was because this other was not meant to be the next in line. They literally were just the object on which this ruler could enact this rite out in public. So that *he* continued to rule them; not Death or those people.

By not allowing Death to move into the next successor's head, this ruler was consigning himself to death, unbeknownst to him. It must have seemed odd to Death that this ruler chose to display this sacred ritual out in the open. And what even puzzled him more, was why this ruler failed to inform him of their plans. Were they not essentially one and the same? Therefore, not only were they by all rights ruling together, but sharing in the decision-making; but also in the implementation of those decisions. And since this ruler was publically demonstrating this was no longer true, then Death was set beside himself, questioning their relationship. Not the mortal; he had made his decision when he enacted this ritual out in the public domain. But how had he done that without Death knowing beforehand? Was he not their spiritual guide? And therefore, was he also not the only spirit which had been internalized (and transferred by all rights) within this family and their dynamics? But apparently not; now there was "this mortal being" defying him. And that was intolerable. Because if Death could not insist that this ruler maintain his part of their agreement, than who would? But that was just it. This individual had a purpose beyond Death, and needing to continue to adhere to this family and their system of succession was out of the question. He desired sole-rulership. And to make that plain, he took this rite of passage as it was intended to be, a sacred rite, and demonstrated for all to see. No secrecy, no covenant: nothing. Complete transparency, but only to the mortal who chose to dramatize the method and dignify it as a form of punishment. Death, however, did not comprehend the significance of this re-enactment until it was too late. But by then, it did not matter to the mortal. He was making a proclamation. But while he was, Death had time to escape that space; but he also chose to return to that ruler's head, with the additional knowledge gained by having done so.

As a spiritual companion it would be quite understandable for Death to be beside himself, since he was not consulted prior to this public display of authority. But was that not the right of the ruler? For them to demonstrate their authority, did they not need to show people who the ruler was? And to do that without consulting another? Not even this spiritual presence? Showing what they were made of, not Death. But with this mortal in particular, ruling their people became utmost; and this dismayed Death.

Death had never been "bested" in this way before. He thought he was ruling along with this human, but that was not the case with this ruler. When this mere mortal took the initiative, and chose not to consult him pre-exhibition, this not only showed disobedience to him; but independence. And, of course, this befuddled this spirit, but only temporarily. Once he saw the exhibition and what had taken place, the beheading of a stranger; then he knew who this ruler might become: Larger than Life. And was Life not the other that Death was struggling to become? Because if he could flit from one creature to another, never having to stick around to see what he had or had not accomplished, then that seemed much more desirous than choosing when the next ruler would rule.

Since when did Death need to become anything more than he was, immortalized? Was he not satisfied with what he was doing in this family and with their legacy? Was he not honored enough knowing that he chose them as much as they chose him? Each and every time they called upon him to perform their sacred rite? But that was just it; this mortal chose not to, which meant this mortal knew that what he was about to do was not an enactment of *the* sacred rite. That came with knowing it was the means of transferring power between two autocrats. And this ruler was having none of that. Nothing against Death, but... How was one to know that? How was one to know that this individual ruler was not really enacting this sacred rite? And that Death had not been a party to it? When all one saw was what was taking place in front of them? But was that not when Death did his turn-around? When he saw that this individual ruler was beheading nothing more than a commoner, then Death knew straight-away this ruler had something else in mind; but not before then.

Being informed in this manner was much better than being made a fool of out in public. Only this spirit did not know that this mortal knew that though. The only thought he held in his mind, was puzzlement. Until he saw the action being displayed out in the public domain; then he knew too, which then helped him to further understand this human and possibly their motivation for doing so. But not necessarily all of their intentions after making such a ghastly display of their sacred ritual; because Death was still a part of the "family." And as long as he was known to be, then this mortal ruler did not have to discuss any of their decisions when it came time to deal "death" out, as a form of punishment. So then, why was Death still out-raged about this formal display? This mere mortal was defying him, out in the open, even though this was unbeknownst to the public. And that is why this mortal was doomed when Death made the determination to return to this ruler's head; never being actualized.

He no longer had any choices in these matters, and that further infuriated him. But being encrypted as immaterial also enlightened him as to what kind of ruler he was dealing with. Somebody that was just as powerful as he was. And that should have comforted him to know, but it did not. Instead, what it appeared to do was set them up for all eternity, in-fighting. Good news to the people, right? But it was not. Because, instead of keeping their fights within their family, they chose to induce others, i.e., triangulate them into their formal matters, as though this was the only way in which to gain notoriety; which was better than no reputation or not even being known.

Death was not supposed to need a reputation or to be known outright? In fact, as a spirit he was supposed to remain immaterial, something that floated in and out of one's head, i.e., one's consciousness. So to remain steadfast to this family and their lineage, not only seemed "weird," but also a sign; something was wrong with either their initiation rite or with their personage. Otherwise, why would Death care whose body he enveloped. But it was not he who was enveloping them, it was the mortal. The mortal made the choice to allow him to come into their lives, not him. And that was Death's doing. He made that their choice. Death continued to uphold this part of their agreement; but the mortal apparently did not, because they failed to inform him of their right to make a choice not to inform him of every decision they made when "death" was being doled out.

Death did not need to be consulted when this ruler decided to kill for demonstration purposes, or for that matter, at any other time. When this individual ruler shared their rite of passage out in public that was when Death knew this too. But until then, enacting that rite of passage was mutually exclusive. All the participants in that rite of passage knew what was taking place, so it was consensual. But without Death, then this enactment became "murder" through their birthright; which seemed more than Death could tolerate or withstand. And without him in the public picture, then there was no spiritual significance to dying in this manner. Beheading was beheading was beheading. And once this mortal-ruler made that perfectly clear in that audition, then Death had no more to say (at least that was the hope). Because once this mortal-rule took this family's secret outside, he no longer needed Death's approval; but it was not meant to be needed. Remember? That though is what needed to be cleared too from this ruler's head.

Internally, this ruler was being instructed by this spirit who thought they needed to be included in everything that this mortal did, including decisions which were no longer theirs to make. Yet to make this perfectly clear to this spiritual being, this mortal had to show him they meant business. And to do that, this ruler had to display their accumulated knowledge out in the open *for all to see*. This then informed that spirit what they were up to. But it also solicited the audience in their internalized war, one that only this ruler knew about; so when they chose to do that, i.e., display what they knew to everybody (including this spirit), they were convinced that this was the only way they could separate within this family and their systems' way of in-thinking.

This was a family system with many more autocrats. And just because this mortal-ruler felt or thought very differently than this "family" did not really mean anything, until it was their time to prove they were different. But taking that approach to the outside for them to see first caused more dissension. And how did it do that? By inducing others into their internal affairs first, which was actually quite clever, but it was not unique. It just meant that this ruler had had enough of their former life, and now it was time to move along; that was all, nothing more, nothing less. However, once that ruler had made their rulership known, then no longer were they seen as the mightiest one of all. Not when their technique was used as punishment. But interiorly, when they made that display so obvious, they were also no longer "covered" by this family or their system of government.

They had literally chosen to uncover everything in front of this audience. But the one secret they kept between them: Death was their parting spirit. Meaning that only royalty were beheaded so that their power could be transferred to the next in line; and Death presided over them, no one else did. So though it looked from the outside, they had broken this one vow, they had not. They had remained celibate to Death, and that was very important to this spirit.

After that display, though, and it was made public knowledge that one could be decapitated if they chose to disobey this ruler, then it also seemed to imply that anyone could lose their head. But they had to disobey this ruler first. However, demonstrating their technique for all to see was the just cause, i.e., anyone could copy what this ruler had just done. Simply by beheading another for punishment or to rationalize what they thought was an injury. Because he had inadvertently demonstrated both of these choices out in the open; that is, as their leader, their role-model he was unintentionally telling them that it was "okay" to conduct one's business through the knife. And that was a much simpler command to follow. Until one had to define just when they were "allowed" to copy them.

In this family's system of ruling, there literally was only one rule to follow. And that was, wait your turn. Pretty easy to follow and to abide by. However, when their rite became public and the punishment for a rule that was explicitly stated, "Do not disobey me" then, no one had to wonder what would happen if they broke this very, simply stated rule. They would also know what happened if they disobeyed this ruler, beheading. With me so far? The problem arose when the technique became the center of attention, and though the ritual aspect was long gone, beheading was not. Because once this rite became public and formulized into a punishment for disobeying a decree set out by an ordinary mortal-ruler, than anyone could simply go out and imitate the technique, which was very simple: Cut-off someone else's head, someone who was not of the family or of this group; and do it with the same instrument that this ruler had used. Pretty simple, straight-forward; and really nothing to imitating this ruler, their technique, or the end result, death to someone else.

But for one to copy this enactment exactly knowingly? From beginning to end? That took more than just imitation.

That took knowing what one was doing, and knowing why they were choosing to follow that leader to a "T." They wanted to be exactly like that leader. And to accomplish that, they had to learn how to follow him, no questions asked. Because they were intending to become him; but to do that, they also had to make a vow with Death. This, though, was not explicitly known, now was it? No, apparently not; because that kind of information was only shared among those who were chosen to be the rulers with Death. And this acknowledgment was only known to those who took a vow to be true to him, and no one else. No other spirit was supposed to rule with them or beside them. That was the formal vow that this family and their ancestor had taken a very long time ago. But not knowing that this spirit had partnered with this family (exactly one individual a very long time ago), meant this "individual" was never going to be, or was intended to be, a part of this group. They were by all rights, just an imitation of their current ruler. But that is not so bad, considering this ruler's supposition. They did not want those others, those autocrats pre-determining when it was time to surrender their reign. And they also did not want Death to know how they came to their decisions about death. And lastly, they did not want anybody else to know what they were thinking of doing to their people if they disobeyed them: Using their rite to take away another's life.

And all of this came to light, just because someone else was going to copy the current ruler to a "T." Imagine that?

Was there something wrong with imitating this ruler? Including, their technique? Because were they not taking what they had learned, and using it so that their people could see who they were? They were no long to be seen as a member of that group of people who they learned that technique from. But that was not all. They were also differentiating from them, i.e., as an individual who ruled autocratically still, but they had taken their rite out and used it sanctimoniously: To establish themselves as separate from those others. But also surreptitiously, making it the very first verbalized agreement, i.e., understanding, between this ruler and the people; that is, since they knew from this demonstration of power that this ruler truly meant business, they were also given a choice: Obey him or die. Plain and simple. So who would not want that kind of power and prestige? Or authority? Especially in knowing that someone could take another's life, and not give it a second thought; only that seeing that ruler demonstrate that kind of power out in the public domain, must have meant there was a lot to having that much power and authority in one's hands.

Their words, however, did not hold that much power (or prestige) in them; not until this ruler had to fulfill his part of the "bargain." And that was to behead someone who had heard his decree or had watched his demonstration, and then went right ahead and disobeyed him. However, what was still a mystery was just what act or action resulted in one being beheaded during this ruler's reign. What exactly was an act of defiance to this particular ruler supposed to look like? Because without that knowledge then it seems they could just behead someone "willy-nilly." So, maybe that was the test? One had to concoct or devise a scheme that would result in this ruler chopping off one's head for disobeying them. Or, perhaps it was just the simple act of imitating them? Or, of taking them at their word? That is they were going to murder someone; and it was only a matter of time when they would. So all one had to do was bide their time. No need to press this ruler to show us anymore of his tyranny. Right? But that was just it. If one did not test this ruler to see what "pushed their buttons" then how was one to know what rule was broken. Disobeying them? What did that actually mean to a commoner, an outsider, someone who was not a part of their internal governance? Questioning them and their form of governance was the rule that issued the death sentence. And it took somebody to do this just once, to know that was what caused the first murder to take place post-decree and outdoors. Because before that, these rulers and their autocracy were not open to any kind of questioning, including why it took beheading one another to become the next ruler; that could very well be defined as "blind obedience." And this ruler did not want to abide by or continue to uphold to this understood rule: No way, no how. So when it came time to prove this, they had to murder someone just to prove they were not going to allow anyone to disobey their rule. It was now made explicit: Do not question me. That was the first acknowledged open act of defiance. Then once this was publicly known, one could then literally go about their business, business as usual.

A death was a death was a death, right? Wrong. Once this ruler killed somebody in the name of them, i.e., this individual had actively defied this ruler through simply asking a question, then there was supposed to be no more killings brought about by this kind of open defiance. Only, now what seemed "unanswered" was the question. What question in particular would bring out that kind of cruel and unusual punishment? Only the ruler knew the answer to that one. Right? All we saw was the end result of that individual's defiance. All they had apparently done was openly defy this ruler by asking a simple question. But why should that ensure this individual's death? Because "asking" in this rulership was completely forbidden; one just complied with what one was supposed to do. Remember, there was no asking? One did just as they were told, internally and externally. That was a part of their formal agreement between their selves. But this ruler took that to mean, he too needed to keep this as a part of their "new" governorship. Not a bad idea when one is only talking about governing from a top-down, perhaps militaristic model. But if one is also trying to break free of this family and their legacy? Then continuing this kind of rulership also seemed to mean one was just lateralizing their rule; which they were. They were self-serving, right? Taking what they knew to be the best way to govern, and using that as their new way to govern their people.

The audience, however, did not know how strict this ruler was until they literally followed-up with their formal agreement that they had made with their people. Then they all knew that he would. Now they knew this despot was not to be questioned, ever. Assuring them that what this ruler meant was what this ruler meant; no questions asked. And now that this was clarified through this ruler's actions, it now became the next rule that one was supposed to follow: One was now forbidden from questioning their ruler or they would lose their head. Yet, if this individual had not openly questioned (i.e., defied) this ruler, then we would not know how they had lost their head; and additionally, what we needed to be aware of so we did not lose ours. Now, no questioning him, and no disobeying him, then no one worry about losing their heads to this ruler. But it seemed such a shame that one had to learn this additional clarification of his rulership the only way he knew how to inform us, through beheading "the criminal." Though it just happened to be someone who just happened to ask him a question, and he happened to interpret it as an injustice to him. Which it was considering this ruler stated outright, no one was to disobey him, even though we did not know asking was not allowed, or that this was a crime in his eyes. We only knew not to disobey him up to this point in time.

Now that we knew questions were not allowed, we could rest easy, right? Wrong, and probably "dead wrong," no pun intended. Once it became obvious that this form of rulership was a, whoever crosses me will die a certain death, then we knew for certain what it meant to disobey him: Do not ask. Simple enough. However, if the only means that this ruler had for executing their power and their authority to rule over us was through execution, and then making it known what it was that this individual did to deserve that form of punishment, then maybe, just maybe, we could become convinced this was the way to be ruled; to be governed over. But this would not last for very long. Because once this ruler demonstrated their technique out in the open for handling disobedience, then those of us in the audience could choose to abide by this form of tyranny, or simply choose not to. Seems simple and straight-forward, does it not? Each time someone was beheaded then we knew why. They had chosen to cross this ruler. And he had followed through with what he agreed to do, punish them for doing so. But was this not a bit extreme? Absolutely!

It only took one observation to note how lethal the punishment was. And if that was not enough, then all one had to do to ascertain how lethal that was, was to ask a simple question. Then one knew for certain how lethal the procedure was, but so was the ruler. We saw that he meant to harm those who disobeyed him; that was made perfectly clear when he beheaded that individual who questioned him. This then brought forth another decree, an exclamation: No one was to ask him a question. Not if they did not value their life. But if one chose to value "life" then their only option was not to follow this ruler: His words or his actions. Then they knew at some point they would be beheaded. However, there were others in this audience who wanted to rule just like this ruler did. They conformed to his actions, and they even followed him word for word.

They went out as instructed and beheaded whomever they felt challenged their authority. And they even enacted the whole scene before they beheaded them: decreeing that this individual disobeyed them, and that they had also asked a simple question. In this sequence exactly; and they could do this without thinking, because they were just simply mimicking their ruler. But the irony was that at one time this was allowed in the name of their ruler. So there really was no learning taking place, now was there? They simply were enacting what had taken a long time ago. Imagine that? History just seems to keep repeating itself, ad nausea here. However, let us suppose one chose to defy their past, just as this ruler did? But this was not known to those who were a part of the audience. In fact, no one knew this except this ruler and Death. Right? And Death did not actually know this until this ruler demonstrated their sacred rite out in the public domain. And then he did not realize the significance of this ruler's actions (or his words) until he made the decision to return to this ruler's head. Then Death knew this ruler was conceiving of doing more with his rulership than those others who came before him. However, as with any family ritual there were still "kinks" to be worked out. Such as, if this ruler was going to deal out death to every individual who happened to cross his authority, then when was Death going to have his turn? Especially, if this ruler seemed bent on being the only ruler who beheaded his fellow human beings?

Mortals sure have a very strange way of working out their problems, do they not? But Death did too. Death wanted to rule just as much, if not more than these mortals. But he also needed them more than they needed him, which fired him up. Because he needed their physicalness to make his presence known, and without them to enact their ritual when it was time for him to say so, then he felt inadequate; which added to the disgruntlement he still had with this mortal being, who seemed to not even care if this spirit remained with him or not. This though was a part of the problem. Once one had materialized inside of a human being, then they were one, literally. There was no separating them until this spirit said it was time, and then he was to alert each partner that it was time. And once they were alerted then each one was to submit to his wishes: die by the hand of the former ruler. Simple, straight-forward, and no need to upset this legacy; and so far, this ruler had done just as he was supposed to, except that he had taken their religious rite outside and used it sanctimoniously, i.e., for their purposes only, no one else's including Death's. In fact, what this subject-ruler did was not at all that abnormal, except they had exercised their powers outside the seclusion of this group and their agreement with Death. However, when this ruler chose to do that, he tipped the scale in favor of himself; not his "brethren" or anyone else. But he did this, because he desired to rule alone; and he meant to continue to do that, despite Death.

Once upon a time, there were scruples. These were informally agreed upon rules which everyone was supposed to abide by including this ruler. However, when this ruler went out of his way to defy them all; and he chose to do so publicly, then it looked to Death as though he was disgracing them all. And he was. This mortal-ruler was instructing the audience that if they defied him, then he would enact their sacred rite. And upon raising the axe to begin beheading this other that is when Death materialized, but then he also realized he had made a tremendous mistake. He had begun to transfer this ruler's power and authority to this other, then recognized this other was not supposed to become the next ruler. Quite ironic that a spirit of this making would not know firsthand what this mortal being was doing. But even more so, what this ruler intended to do prior to their first enactment of their sacred rite. But since he did not know that at the time, but knew so subsequently, was that also why Death still felt unrequited?

Death had not had an opportunity since that ruler-mortal began their rule to make any decisions regarding "their time." And that was a major problem for Death. Because he was the one who held that knowledge, and he knew when it was time to enact it. But by having to wait until then, he simply grew restless. But this "restlessness" was new to him. And that meant when that ruler-mortal broke their formal agreement with that ruling class, they also broke their sacred promise to succeed their power when Death deemed it was time. Otherwise, why would Death feel this way? Right? So his restlessness was legitimate; he knew it was their time, and this ruler-mortal chose to ignore him, just as he had when he made that earlier decision (without Death's knowledge) to break from the family and their formal arrangement. Which only meant one thing to Death: he had to figure out how to abscond this ruler-mortal, i.e., convince him to surrender to Death (but to return to his family). And he had to do so quickly. Time was of the essence, and he was the only one apparently who knew this.

Remember when this spirit made the decision to return to this mortal's head? That was the very first time *he knew* what they were doing. Because, before that he was basically just complying with their original arrangement: Beheading only took place when it was time for a succession to take place. And he was the only one who knew when that was supposed to transpire. But when he saw what this ruler was doing, and to whom, then he perceived "his error." And that made him uncomfortable, at first. Nevertheless, it also forced him to take stock, i.e., look at what this mortal was doing. Not only enacting their sacred rite in front of all these people, but *he* was making that possible; not Death nor the family from whence they came. And if this mortal could that? Then it also meant this ruler-mortal had something this spirit deemed he should know.

Informed now, Death saw he had no other choice but to return to this mortal's head. But he did so, with a plan. This plan had very different features in it. In fact, it was much grander than the earlier one. And unfortunately for us mortals, when Death re-entered this mortal's body, he kept what he knew from this individual too, tit for tat. This evening out, though, did not help those of us who did not know what it meant to be triangulated; that was new to us. Especially, since all we saw taking place right in front of us was this ruler displaying their technique to us, followed by the decree – this will happen to you good people if you do not obey me. That one beheading was enough for us lowly subjects to know what we needed to do: obey them or simply choose not to. And know that there would now be a punishment doled out if we chose not to obey him: we would lose our heads to this ruler. But it was even made more certain, death that is, when that poor fool asked a simple question; which looked to us on the outside as "clarification." But internally to this ruler (and Death) as an affront to their authority; and so, the consequence for that was the same as disobeying them, beheading.

Enough, right? Wrong. Though it looked as though Death and this mortal had worked out their inner differences among their selves, they had not. For one, there were no differences for them to work-out until this individual decided to break free from the family. And once they did that was when Death was "blind-sided." By this very action though, it was telling Death they were no longer needed, esoterically either.

This mortal knew even at this rudimentary level what they were doing; they literally were breaking a covenant: A group of secret keepers. And to break free of them, meant surrendering to Death and his wishes, i.e., on his command they would have to give up their rulership, and transfer it the next in line. And all those within this sacred group knew this and they knew how that was supposed to happen, under Death's watchful eye. Yet, when this mortal made that singular decision, to take what they knew out into the open, and demonstrate it for all to see, *without Death knowing what they were doing,* then the rite itself became secular: a form of punishment for disobeying this very ordinary ruler.

This covenant of autocrats (strange as that may sound now), does not sound that strange at all. Especially, when this particular group and their pact depended on the individual to stay with them, never straying from their norm or their ways, and this included never even thinking about taking anything outside the home. And this individual ruler did: he took their sacred rite out and used it without their permission to do so. And internally, i.e., within this individual's mind, he had shut the door on Death. Literally keeping him from knowing his plans; but when he chose to do this, he was also keeping all of them in the covenant from knowing what he was up to. Because Death was their conduit, their spirit, and since he was the one who informed them when it was time to die and succeed, it also meant he could portend. But it also meant this spirit also had the power to know when he was supposed to stop him. If he could portend death, then by all rights he should know what this mortal-ruler was going to do, i.e., defy them. That was his job, right? So to shut him out at this level, this internal one was the best tactical maneuver he could create at the time. For the simple reason that, it not only kept Death from his job, but also from perceiving what this mere mortal was planning to do. But, it also transformed this individual. That simple act of keeping Death from portending also formed a boundary around this individual; which helped him stay focused on his plans, and it intentionally disrupted that inner connection to those who were on the outside of him. All this internal work, not only significantly changed him, but also made him seem different to these others, which also added to the haste felt by Death.

The anxiety backwash

This much determination must have started somewhere, right? But where exactly? If they were supposed to be deeply connected to one another through Death, then how did this individual learn how to silence him? And do so with a definite. That mere mortal must have learned how to do this in their mind. But how had they? All they had was practical knowledge, i.e., watching others go through their sacred rite without a word. In fact, from an observer's point of view, their performing their sacred rite looked as if it was all conducted as planned. And it was. But as each succession took place, there had to be a sign, a premonition that it was their turn to enact this rite. Otherwise, how would they know internally that it was their time to rule? And, also know their sign? That is, what informed them Death was beginning their rite? Was it a sound or a symbol? Something which was out of the ordinary, which they could depend on was Death telling them it was either: their time, and it had come to an end; or it was their time to move into that former ruler's place. And their time would begin once again.

Yet, this individual chose to break-free of this family and their legacies before Death could enact this rite of passage with him post his initiation into their rulership. And yet, he was still present in this mortal's physical body when he initiated. That is correct. Their physical enactment of that rite, out in the open air, caused more than just another's head to be taken. It literally caused Death to out himself in public invisibly, just before that life was taken. So even though this new leader was enacting their ritual, impartially, Death and this mortal's body were still one; as it was pre-ordained to be. That is they were still bond by the physicalness of the body, but they were no longer together.

Earlier this mortal had deliberately parted with Death (when he was making plans to leave the family's home with their secret). So when that mortal physically moved their arm, raising it in the way that Death knew, it prompted him to come forward, but from there; not from out of this mortal's head. So when that arm was moved, "readied," it literally signaled to Death it was time, however he also assumed that this mortal was still associated to that family and their rite. This then prompted Death to become visible in that arm. He could then see and feel what this mortal-ruler was doing, enacting their sacred rite out in public. And that was enough. It was enough for Death to acknowledge that this ruler-mortal knew what they were doing, and that he had nothing to do with that decision.

Defeated, now, Death made his first decision in a very long time: He retreated. But with an image and something new, a muscle memory; this was much different than how he had known before. For one, he did not know this human had sent him away, i.e., out of his head, and into another part of its body. And two, now that he knew this, he also learned what that meant: when that arm was raised, it was time to behead someone. And if Death wanted to partake in this, he had better return to that place; otherwise that human would conduct that ritual without him. So back he went. But he did not do this without taking with him one more "addition." The image of that raised arm readied to strike the blow that would bring certain death to that individual. And with this knowledge, Death not only knew more about this mortal than before, but also what that image meant from a spiritual perspective. One could literally take a life without having to think about it. But also do so without any cause whatsoever, i.e., just for demonstration purposes. However, just because Death thought this was what the human was doing when they were enacting their rite, it did not mean that was what this mortal was planning to do.

The mortal-ruler thought he was performing this act completely solo, so was not even thinking about Death. Or even what that arm being raised in that manner might mean to Death: to begin his part of the ritual enactment. And because he was so focused on the act, he had also made the fatal mistake of thinking that Death was no longer with him because he had banished him from his mind. And because he had, he did not think there was any reason to be concerned about his presence, or that Death would be anywhere near him or even housed within him. Especially since the only time he knew of him was when it was time to succeed; and since that was not what this enactment was, then Death should not have been present. But he was. He was there in that arm. And the mortal-ruler did not even notice.

Given the type of relationship these two had that should not have come as much of a surprise, but it did to Death. Because, as was mentioned earlier, he thought he was in the head of this mortal; not in his arm, and this seemed rather peculiar to him. For a spirit to be intentionally re-placed to a part of the body which had nothing to do with the mind, seemed outrageous and more than just humiliating. It seemed downright discriminating. And it was. For Death to be present (and not in that human's mind or psyche) only meant one thing to Death, he had been moved to a peripheral location which was thought to be lesser than his original home: The place where most believe "power" and "authority" stem from, the brain. So when he realized he had been re-housed in the next logical location, i.e., the arm which held the instrument, Death should have felt this was an equitable shift. But he did not. In fact, when it came time to deliver the blow which caused Death to be summoned, so death could be dealt, he not only did not know why he was being called forth from that peculiar place; but also why it was better to be summoned from there, then nowhere at all. But that kind of logic only incited Death. It caused him to be aware of his surroundings (something which neither this mortal nor Death had to acknowledge before), and also to look at what they were doing prior to committing their act; which as Death noted, was not their ritual act. But it was a significant part of it. But it also led to more questions about why a spirit such as Death would recognize all of these, rather than the human.

Was it not the human who had intentionally moved this spiritual presence out of their mind so that when it came time to enact their plans, they could do so uninterrupted? And since that was what this mortal had done, then why was Death's re-location to that particular area of the body such an ordeal for him? To be located anywhere other than this human's mind-brain was a lesser than position for this spirit, and that was not to be tolerated. But appearing in that arm also seemed to mean he was of no use to this mortal-ruler. This was quite demoralizing to this spirit (to say the least); especially since he had a history with this family of individuals. And now that he was no longer in this human's mind-brain, not only was this a demotion, it also showed Death who was the boss. And it surely was not him. Because, if he was not in this mortal's head or their arm then Death would be "out," there would be no place for him in this human's body. And that was the worst scenario for this spirit, since he needed their bodies more than he was ready to acknowledge.

Death was not of the mind to remain in that part of that human's body for long. In fact, to remain there would be a "death sentence" for him. So then that meant Death had to make another choice, an informed decision based on where he wanted to be located. If not in the head or the arm, then where? And he needed to make this decision rather quickly, once he returned to that arm after having verified that what was taking place was not their ritual act, but a simulation of it. How much time did he have to remain in that upper arm, before this mortal knew he was there? And if he chose to remain in that mortal's arm so he could be party to the follow through, i.e., what that human had begun to enact when that arm was raised, then what would happen next? The movement of that arm as it was being raised (which is when he was summoned), not only signaled Death to come out and see what was taking place, but it also located him in this mortal's body. And if he had not materialized in this mortal's upper arm as he did, then we would not know he was there; but neither would this mortal. And since "we" know that he is there, we also share in his vision. We can see that arm raised and readied to deliver the final blow. And we also know that when that action is finalized, it will not only kill the subject, but it will also inform us of what that kind of action can do. So when we saw Death in that arm, and Death saw what that mortal was doing with that arm raised as it was, then we could all see that mortal enacting their rite. But it was not just this; it was also that we could literally see what killing another literally looked like through beheading. And if this was not bad enough, this arm action and Death's part in it also had other consequences, associations attached to it too.

Murder, for one; but also dismembering another human being seemingly just for demonstrating one's might. These were, however, considered to be two of the most heinous acts that a human (with a spiritual presence) could be involved in. And what was even worse, was that since we knew this we were also just as "guilty" as these people, i.e., those who actually enacted these "rites" right in front of us, even if it was for instructional purposes. Because, as long as we stood by and just watched, then not only were we actively participating in their production, but we were also enabling them. Keeping their secret about what they were doing between us. They were enacting their rite with the caveat that it was a punishment brought about by disobedience. Not for the right to succeed into a new position. And now that we knew this, then we should obey them without ever asking why, or "how come." In fact, by showing us what they could do without a moment's hesitation, they not only were guaranteeing our silence, but this ruler "doubled that" with the next beheading. And when he did that, then we should have known that this ruler knew exactly what he was capable of, even if Death was not supposed to be there; that is in his mind.

Now that Death was in that upper arm, and was culpable in both beheadings, we knew we had to devise a plan to eradicate Death and this human's arm simultaneously. Because without either Death or that arm, then this human was helpless; they no longer were a threat, but neither was this spirit. And if one could eliminate both in a single blow, then why not? Why not stop this human from killing or dismembering another human being? Because that would mean having to enact their rite, or something very similar to it; but to do that meant one had to literally imitate them. And that was much worse than just being complacent, or being a silent partner, a colluder. Because by imitating them, not only was there the fear one would become just like them, but also that when one imitated them they too would know the power that came from taking another's life against their will. This was a major distinction between this ruler's use of their skills on the outside, and how they were supposed to be used within this family of individuals.

Within their rulership, when one beheaded another there was a sense of duty and honor in this kind of taking; which was completely absent when this mortal-ruler went out and demonstrated this to the people. Plus, when this ruler chose a subject (against their will) for their demonstration, then not only was there no honor in their death, but also no reason as such for their death. Other than to show us how powerful they were as a family member who knew how to behead another. And because they held this power inside, this individual could also perform this act without too much thought when it came time for them to kill their predecessor; which was how this act was supposed to be performed on the inside. But when taken outside of this venue and into the public domain, then it became just another killing. However, for those who were watching this demonstration for imitation purposes, it became more than just that; it became permission to be just like them. Because when that ruler showed us what he could do, and he did this without much thought given to the action, then it became very apparent that beheading another in front of others was the best method to invite fear. Which in our minds, equated to power; and the power to take another's life without their say-so, seemed even better than inducing fear in another (since this "after-effect" did not remain very long in the collective conscious). And since we were looking for sustaining power, and not necessarily fear this made perfect sense to us.

How could this mortal (and Death) be this powerful? Especially since all they did was behead one another? And they had done so for such a long time and in silence. But now that this ruler-mortal broke their silence and showed us what they had been doing since their earliest beginnings, we too now knew what it was like to be one of them; but we lacked one "thing," Death. And without Death, not only would we not have to remember theirs was a ritual act done out of respect for order; but that not having any idea about Death, or why it was important to remember his presence, then we too could be just like this ruler-mortal; someone who only cared about power, and establishing one's authority through fear and discontent. Only that was the "secret."

This human knew that what he was doing was not their sacred rite. And because he knew this, and thought nobody else did, he was safe with their secret. But he was not. Not only did Death know that this ruler-mortal was not enacting their rite, but we knew this too. Death needed to be present for that rite to be enacted as it was supposed to be, but the recipients of that rite were supposed to be family members. So that all three of them could perform this archaic rite just as it was supposed to be; and do so knowing which side of the rite one was on. One was either on the accepting end, and they were the one taking that other's life, or they were submitting their rulership to this other, so they could continue their legacy. And Death was mitigating this ritual or presiding over it as the case may be. Once that individual ruler broke from their family and displayed their skillset out in public, this formal understanding was completely abolished. Which also meant that without these three in place, then what was taking place in front of us was nothing more than a punishment, and a very cruel and unusual one at that. So then, why would we want to repeat what we were watching, especially if we thought that their actions were cruel and unusual? And also without those three elements, what was the purpose for severing one's head? If not to also be seen as one of them; and so since we were not supposedly one of them (nor did we appear to want to be just like them), then why would we want to continue their behavior. Unless, we too believed beheading was the only means one had to keep one under control. And so, if we chose to replicate it without Death or the ritual aspect, then not only were we learning how to control another through this means, but death too. And if that was not enough, we also now had the means and the wherewithal to imitate that human exactly; just by watching that one enactment.

Now that Death and the ritual aspect were no longer a part of this demonstration, there no longer seemed to be any novelty in this one activity. Beheading was beheading was beheading. However, just because they had shared this with us, it still remained a mystery as to why one would want to even think about imitating them. In fact even contemplating the thought to do so, seemed heinous, and would most certainly bring death to us, i.e., those of us who were watching that demonstration take place out in public. So unless we really desired to be one of them (i.e., the ruler), and were willing to do the worst act one could ever conceive of (kill another just to prove how powerful one could be), then we had better not follow them. Because after that mortal-ruler came out and showed us what they and their family had been doing for years - conducting this ritual act upon their selves – we, in the viewing audience, should have learned what it meant to be one of them. And also what having that kind of knowledge housed in one's insides did to them: It literally tore them apart, instead of sealing them together. And that should have been enough to warn us away from this peculiar family and their dynamics; but it did not. Now, why might that be? Because in their disclosure they were inadvertently empowering us; by showing us exactly what it was like to be one of them. Someone who could raise their arm, summon Death, and then bring down that selfsame arm finalizing what they had set out to do: kill someone. And then think nothing of it, except that it was a means to prove how powerful one was. But this simple demonstration was not enough to dissuade the questioner. In fact, they took it upon their self to question this peculiar mortal-ruler after that demonstration and after that decree;

which seemed rather peculiar, in light of what just took place in front of us.

This could only mean this individual did not know what that ruler-mortal really was capable of, or they simply did not know what being disobedient meant. But how was one to know, without asking? And asking the individual who just happened to lay that law down for the very first time? Especially since none of us in the audience knew what disobeying them meant. So when that individual subject did just that, and they lost their head because of it, then we all knew something more about that ruler-mortal. We knew they had a hair-pin trigger, and they responded to it as a reflex. Almost as though they too only knew how to do this, and nothing more. And who the heck would want that kind of trigger-happy presence ruling anyone? Let alone a group of people who just happened to be watching this entire scene unfold like a dream right in front of them.

Some dream, huh? Only it was not a dream, was it? But that was what it seemed to appear to be, watching as that mortal-ruler took another's head in a matter of minutes after just showing us what they were more than capable of. So why had that questioner asked that ruler-mortal what disobeying them meant? And then lost their head due to this very innocent act? Because before this, questioning was unheard of, but so was disobedience; and so when both of these came out of that one individual, and out in the open in front of all these people, then it was no wonder this mortal-ruler responded as they did. They were projecting onto this simple act of inquiry too much of themselves; and when they did, they not only showed us the ugliest side of humanity one could possibly imagine, but their intolerance to any sense of "other" worth. Then it became self-evident that what we were really up against was not just this mortal-ruler's "breaking out," but their inability to deal with anything other than what they had set out to do: Ensure they were ruling, no questions asked.

Remember when picking up a stick or a stone to defend oneself was better than no defense at all? Especially when one finally recognized what they truly were up against: rulers who seemed "hell-bent" on doing what they set out to do, and had turned a blind eye to everything else, except what they needed. Sound familiar? No? Well, then, here is a clue: Oh Death! Now where could he be?

Bibliography

Battles, D. A., & Hudak, J. (2005). Exploring the Interrelationships of Art and Geology through a course module on European Ice Age Cave Art. *Journal of Geoscience Education*, 176-183.

Lopez-Pedraza, R. (2000). *Dionysus in exile: On the repression of the body and emotion.* Wilmette, Illinois: Chiron Publications.

Marshack, A. (1996). A Middle Paleolithic symbolic composition from the Golan Heights: The earliest known depictive image. *Current Anthropology*, 357-365.